This book belongs to:

Table of Contents

Table of Contents

Unit 1 Beginning Letter Sounds

1 Say the letter at the beginning of the row out loud.
Circle the objects that begin with that letter sound.

a) **d**

b) **j**

c) **q**

d) **m**

e) **p**

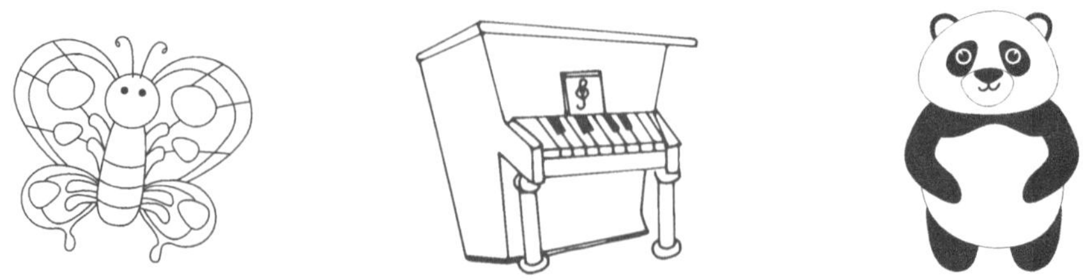

Beginning Letter Sounds (cont.)

2 Say the name of the object out loud.
Match the object to its **beginning letter sound**.

a) 

b) 

c) 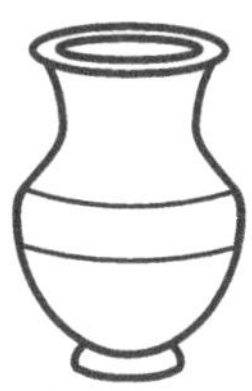

d) 

e) 

v

b

f

w

y

Beginning Letter Sounds (cont.)

3. Say the name of the object out loud.
Colour the **beginning letter sound** for the object's name.

a) 

p	a

b) 

t	g

c) 

i	n

d) 

r	h

e) 

s	c

f) 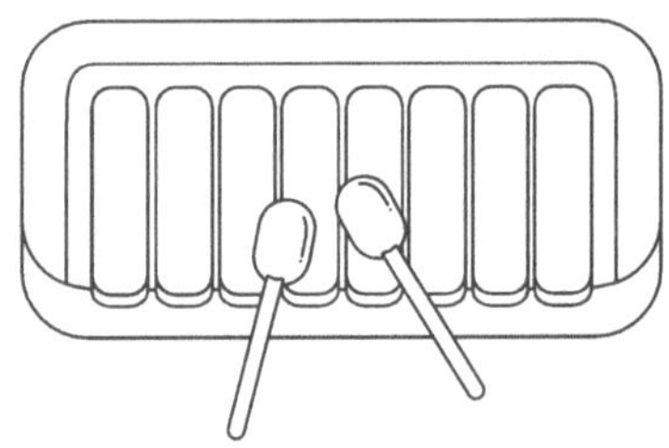

t	x

g) 

l	u

h) 

g	n

i) 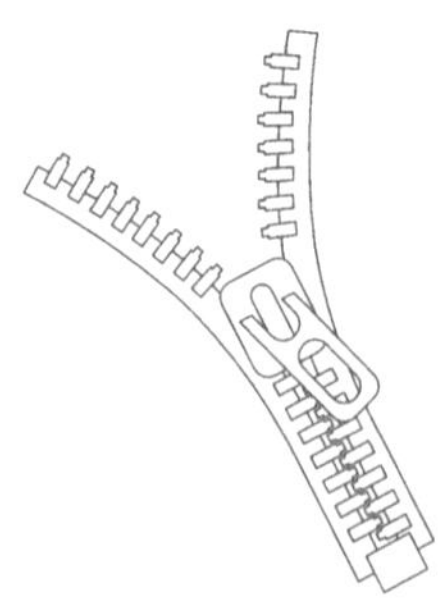

k	z

Beginning Letter Sounds (cont.)

4. Say the name of the object out loud.
Colour the **beginning letter sound** for the object's name.

a)

g	c

b)

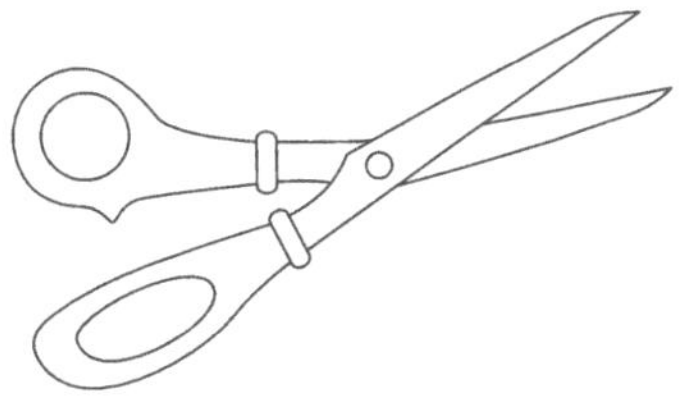

s	t

c)

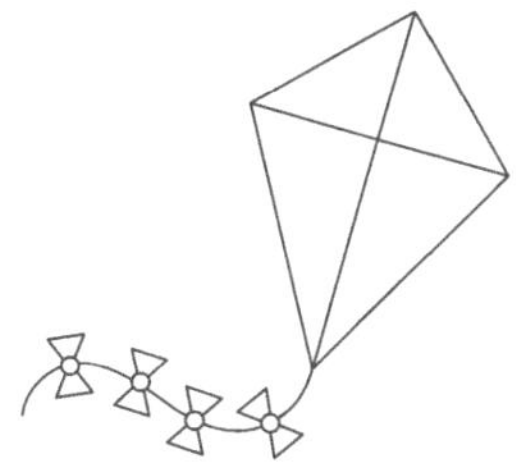

w	k

d)

n	r

e)

b	a

f)

n	m

g)

j	l

h)

e	d

i)

h	o

Beginning Letter Sounds: Rhyming

1 Change the letter that makes the **beginning letter sound**. Print the new rhyming word on the line.

a) Change **bat** to 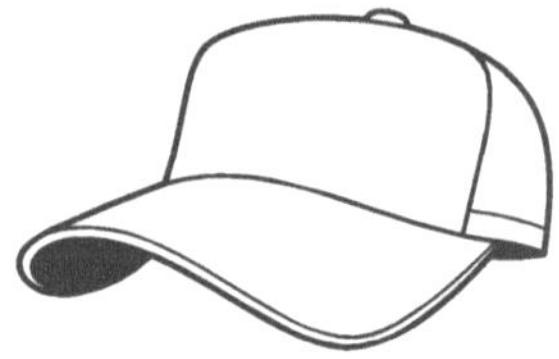

b) Change **hen** to 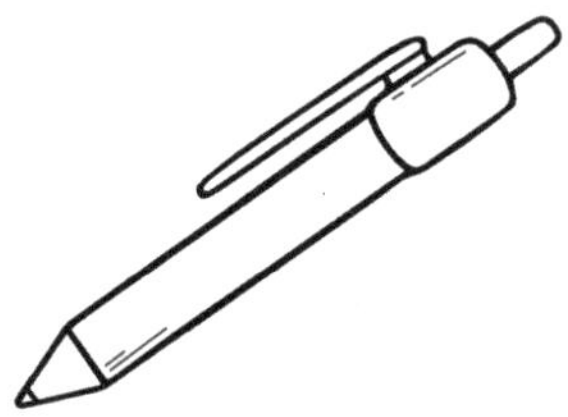

c) Change **hit** to 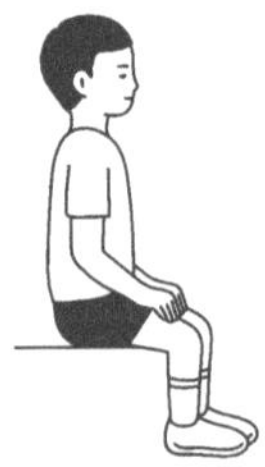

d) Change **mug** to 

e) Change **log** to 

Beginning Letter Sounds: Rhyming (cont.)

2 Change the letter that makes the **beginning letter sound**. Print the new rhyming word on the line.

a) Change **red** to 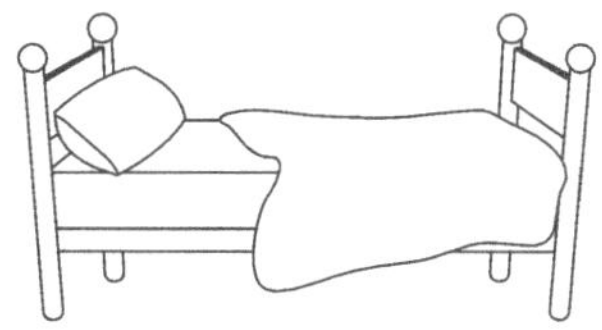 ____________

b) Change **jar** to  ____________

c) Change **big** to  ____________

d) Change **hot** to  ____________

e) Change **fun** to  ____________

Ending Letter Sounds

1 Say the name of the object out loud.
Colour the **ending letter sound** for the object's name.

a)

l m

b)

g t

c)

t r

d)

b x

e)
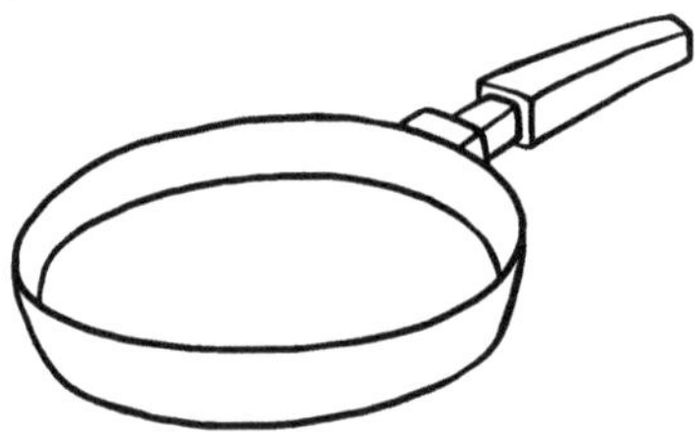
n s

f)

d l

g)

y k

h)

f m

i)

r p

Ending Letter Sounds (cont.)

2. Say the name of the object out loud. Print the letter that shows the **ending letter sound** for the object's name. Choose from the letters on the right.

a)  boo

b)  wel

c)  bir

d) 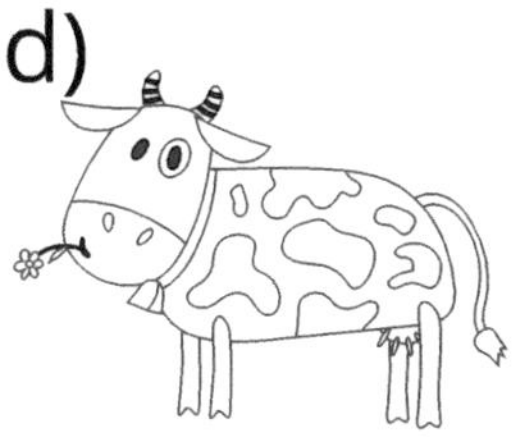 co

e)  cra

l
d
k
b
w

Beginning and Ending Letter Sounds

Say the name of the object out loud. Complete the word by printing the **beginning and ending letter sounds**.

1

__a__

2

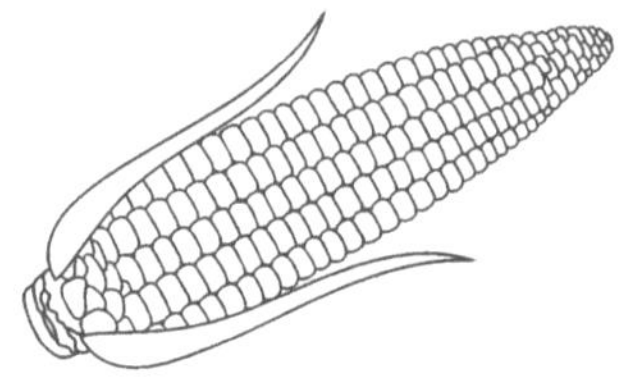

__or__

3

__io__

4

__e__

5

__ea__

6

__oo__

Unit 3

Consonant Blends

s blends

scarf 

skunk 

sled 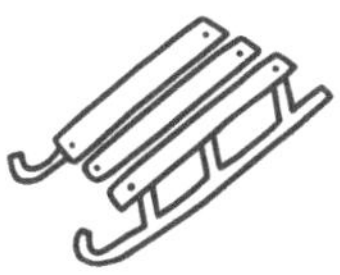

smile 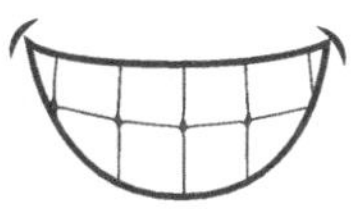

snail 

sponge 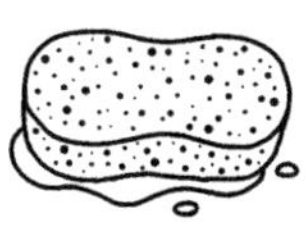

stool 

swan 

r blends

broom 

crab 

dress 

frame 

grapes 

present 

truck 

l blends

blanket 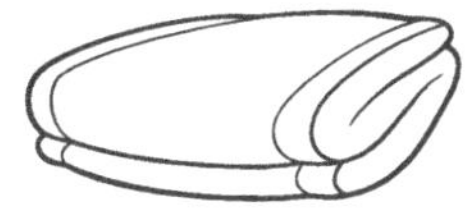

cloud 

flag 

glue 

planet 

Consonant Blends with s

1 Say the name of the object out loud.
Colour the correct **consonant blend** for the object's name.

a) 

sc	sm

b) 

st	sn

c) 

sp	sm

d) 

st	sp

e) 

sc	sl

f) 

sk	st

g) 

sn	sl

h) 

st	sc

i) 

sl	sk

Colour the sc words. red
Colour the sn words. blue
Colour the sp words. green
Colour the st words. yellow
Colour the sl words. purple
Colour the sk words. orange

Consonant Blends with s (cont.)

2. Say the name of the object out loud.
Colour the correct **consonant blend** for the object's name.

a) 

sw	sl

b) 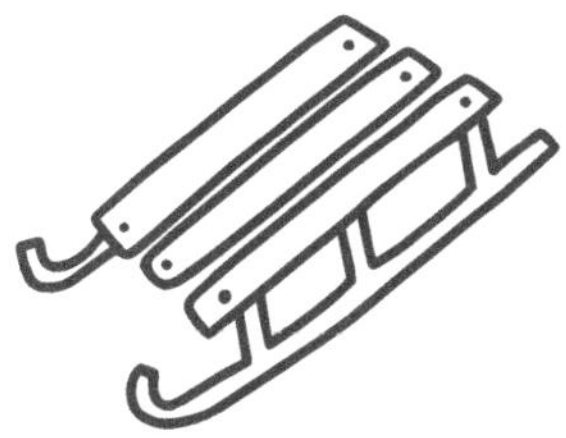

sl	st

c) 

sp	sn

d) 

sn	st

e) 

sk	sm

f) 

sn	sw

g) 

sk	sp

h) 

sn	sm

i) 

st	sl

Colour the sw words. pink
Colour the sl words. purple
Colour the sn words. blue
Colour the st words. yellow
Colour the sk words. orange
Colour the sm words. grey

Consonant Blends with *s* (cont.)

3 Read the sentence.
Fill in the blank with a **consonant blend** from the box.

sc	sl	sm	sn	sp	st

a) I sit on the ______ool .

b) Remi ______ips on the ice.

c) I ______ill my drink.

d) Alice ______ells the flower.

e) ______hool starts tomorrow.

f) The ______ail is slow.

Consonant Blends with *s* (cont.)

4 Read the sentence.
Fill in the blank with a **consonant blend** from the box.

sc	sk	sl	sm	sp	sw

a) The cow has ______ots.

b) I play on the ______ing.

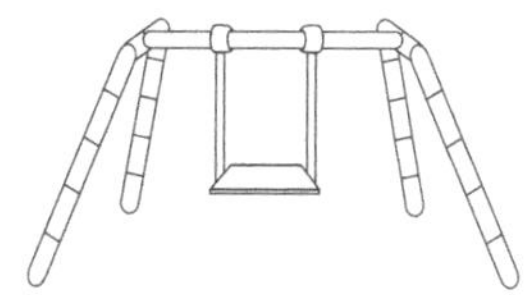

c) Julie buys a new ______arf.

d) There is a ______unk outside.

e) I ______ile when I'm happy.

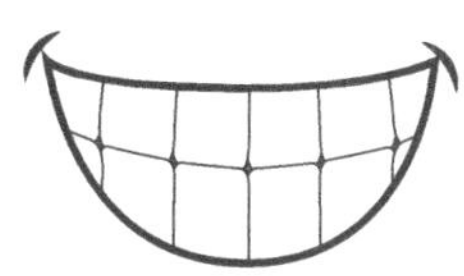

f) I saw a ______oth at the zoo.

Consonant Blends with *r*

1 Say the name of the object out loud.
Colour the correct **consonant blend** for the object's name.

a)

fr | br

b)

tr | dr

c)

br | cr

d)

pr | tr

e)

cr | gr

f)

br | tr

g)

cr | fr

h)

gr | fr

i)

pr | br

Colour the **br** words. pink
Colour the **tr** words. yellow
Colour the **cr** words. orange
Colour the **pr** words. red
Colour the **gr** words. green
Colour the **fr** words. blue

Consonant Blends with *r* (cont.)

2 Say the name of the object out loud.
Colour the correct **consonant blend** for the object's name.

a) 

dr	pr

b) 

cr	tr

c) 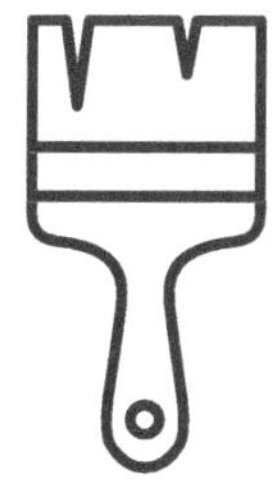

fr	br

d) 

tr	gr

e) 

dr	fr

f) 

pr	cr

g) 

cr	pr

h) 

cr	dr

i) 

br	tr

Colour the **dr** words. red
Colour the **cr** words. blue
Colour the **br** words. green
Colour the **tr** words. yellow
Colour the **fr** words. purple
Colour the **pr** words. orange

Consonant Blends with r (cont.)

3 Read the sentence.
Fill in the blank with a **consonant blend** from the box.

br	cr	dr	fr	gr	pr

a) I ______ess the button.

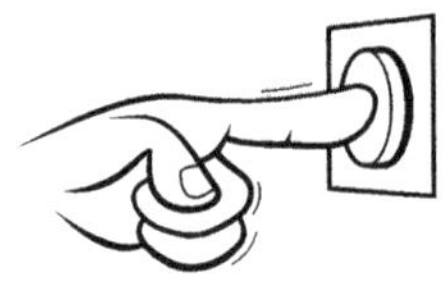

b) The ______ame is for the picture.

c) Use a ______oom to sweep.

d) My ______ink is finished.

e) The ______own is shiny.

f) We cook on the ______ill.

Consonant Blends with r (cont.)

4 Read the sentence.
Fill in the blank with a **consonant blend** from the box.

br	cr	tr	fr	gr	pr

a) We ______y eggs for breakfast.

b) I love ______occoli.

c) The ______ane is very tall.

d) I have a toy ______ain.

e) These ______apes are purple.

f) I can ______int my letters.

Consonant Blends with *l*

1 Say the name of the object out loud.
Colour the correct **consonant blend** for the object's name.

a)
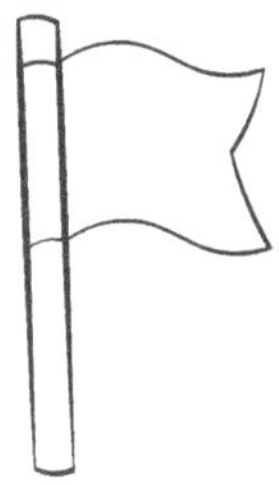

fl	bl

b)

cl	gl

c)

pl	bl

d)

cl	gl

e)
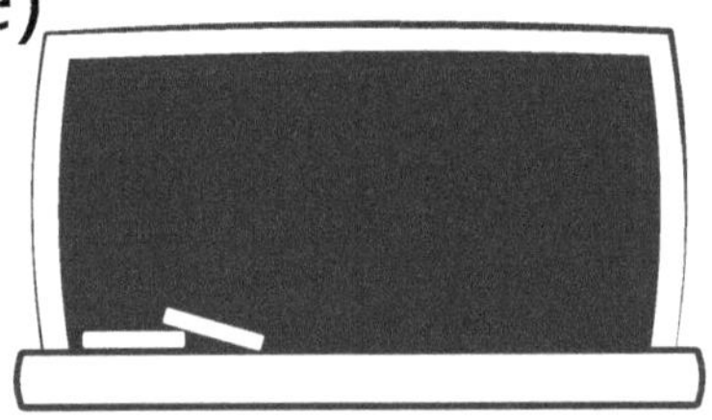

bl	fl

f)

pl	cl

g)
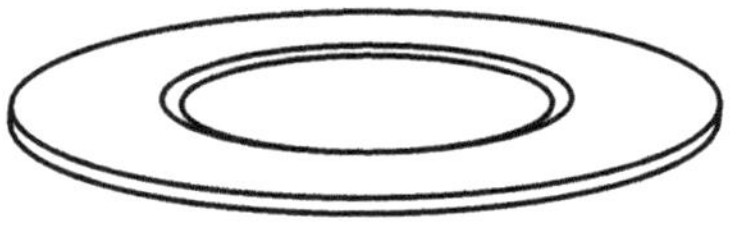

gl	pl

h)
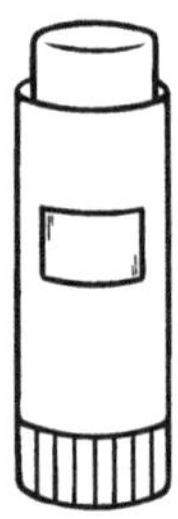

fl	gl

i)

bl	pl

Colour the **fl** words. pink
Colour the **gl** words. yellow
Colour the **pl** words. orange
Colour the **cl** words. red
Colour the **bl** words. green

Consonant Blends with *l* (cont.)

2 Say the name of the object out loud.
Colour the correct **consonant blend** for the object's name.

a) 

bl	cl

b) 

fl	cl

c) 

bl	gl

d) 

fl	cl

e) 

pl	bl

f) 

gl	bl

g) 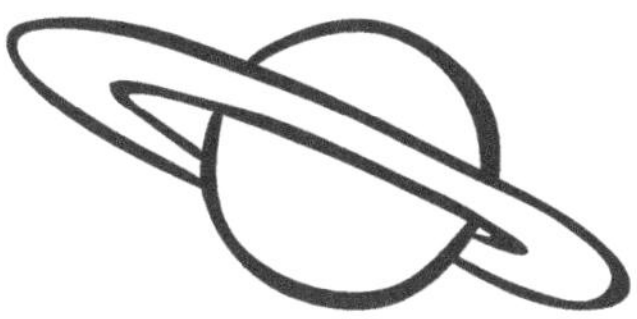

pl	fl

h) 

gl	bl

i) 

fl	cl

Colour the **fl** words. pink
Colour the **gl** words. yellow
Colour the **pl** words. orange
Colour the **cl** words. red
Colour the **bl** words. green

Consonant Blends with *l* (cont.)

3 Read the sentence.
Fill in the blank with a **consonant blend** from the box.

bl	cl	fl	gl	pl

a) My cousin plays the ____ute.

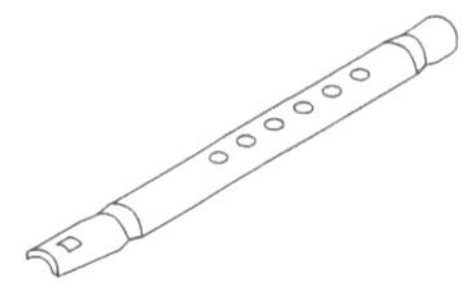

b) The ____anket is cozy.

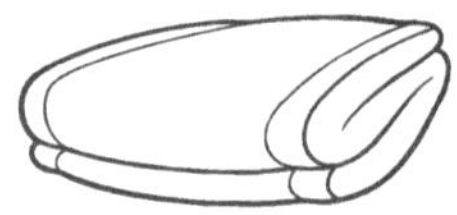

c) My ____ant is growing.

d) The ____itter is sparkly.

e) The ____am lives in the ocean.

f) I ____oss my teeth at night.

Consonant Blends with *l* (cont.)

4 Read the sentence.
Fill in the blank with a **consonant blend** from the box.

bl	cl	fl	gl	pl

a) The ______ock tells time.

b) My ______ower is pretty.

c) I lost my ______ove .

d) The kids ______ay together.

e) The ______ame is very hot.

f) The sky is ______ue .

More Consonant Blends

1 Read the sentence.
Fill in the blank with a **consonant blend** from the box.

cr	fr	gl	pl	sn	sp

a) Gerry colours with a ______ayon .

b) There is a ______ake in the garden.

c) We flew in a ______ane .

d) Eat soup with a ______oon .

e) A ______og lives in the pond.

f) I put on ______oves to warm my hands.

More Consonant Blends (cont.)

2 Read the sentence.
Fill in the blank with a **consonant blend** from the box.

dr	pl	sk	sl	st	tr

a) We took a ______ain on our trip.

b) I like playing on the ______ide.

c) When I'm thirsty I have a ______ink.

d) In winter we ______ate on ice.

e) My mom waters the ______ant.

f) There are a lot of ______ars in the sky.

Unit 4

Words with *sh*

1 Say the name of the object out loud. Draw a line from the object to the matching word. Circle the ***sh*** in the word.

a) 

b) 

c) 

d) 

e) 

ship

fish

shell

sheep

brush

Colour the **ship**. brown

Colour the **fish**. green

Colour the **shell**. pink

Colour the **sheep**. blue

Colour the **brush**. red

Words with *sh* (cont.)

2 Say the name of the object out loud.
Circle the objects that have ***sh*** in their name.

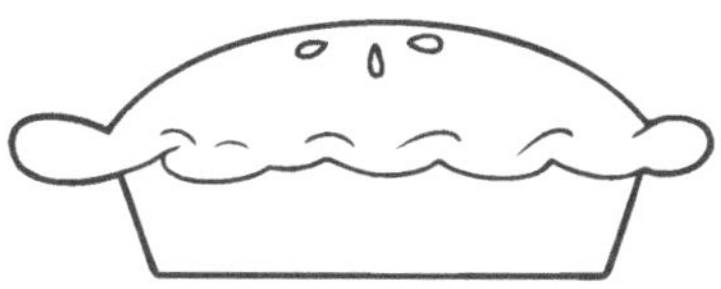

3 Read the sentence.
Fill in the blank with the correct word from the box.

shell	shop

a) I found a ______________ on the beach.

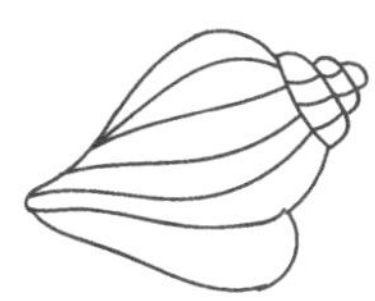

b) The ______________ has candy for sale.

Unit 5

Words with *th*

1 Say the name of the object out loud. Draw a line from the object to the matching word. Circle the ***th*** in the word.

a) 	think
b) 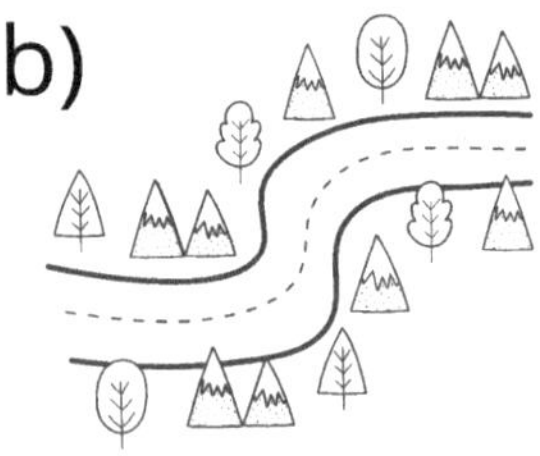	thread
c) 	bath
d) 	thumb
e) 	path

Colour the **thread**. black

Colour the **path**. red

Colour **think**. yellow

Colour the **bath**. blue

Colour the **thumb**. green

Words with *th* (cont.)

2 Say the name of the object out loud.
Circle the objects that have ***th*** in their name.

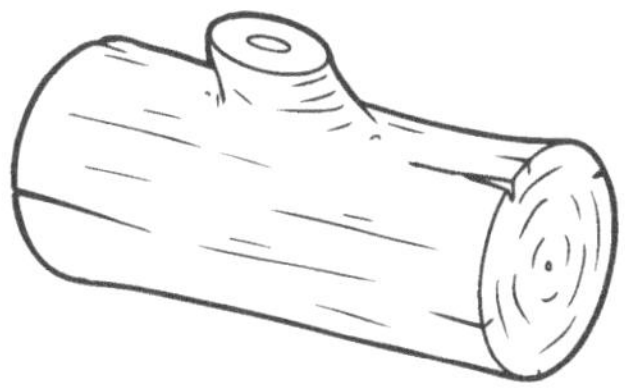

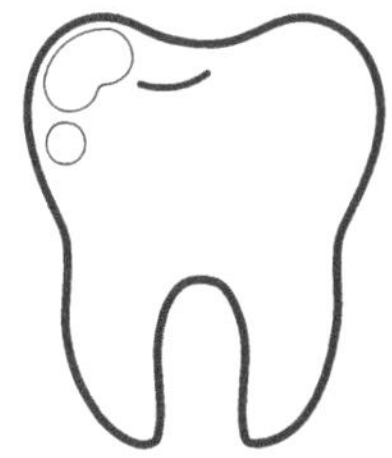

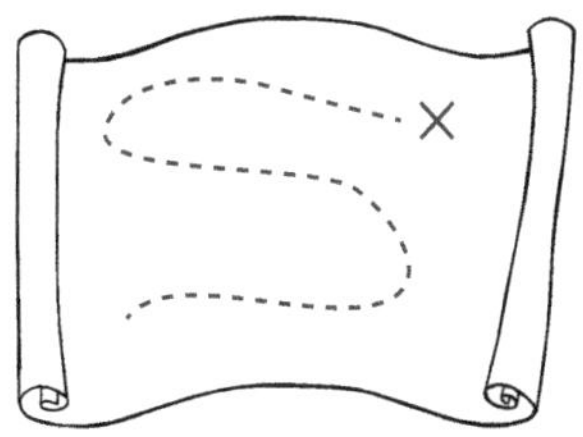

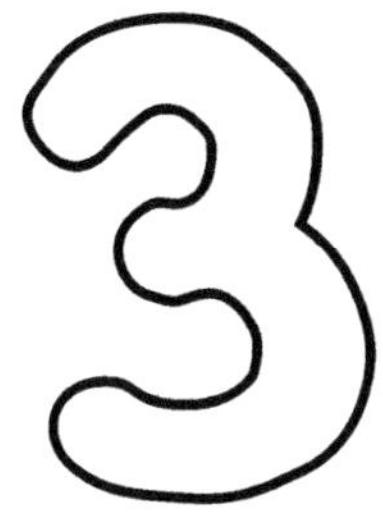

3 Read the sentence.
Fill in the blank with the correct word from the box.

they	with

a) I like to play ______________ my best friend.

b) ______________ have two pet dogs.

Unit 6

Short and Long Vowels

Long vowels say their name. Short vowels make different sounds. Read the examples below. Say the names of the objects out loud.

a

short ă

jam

long ā

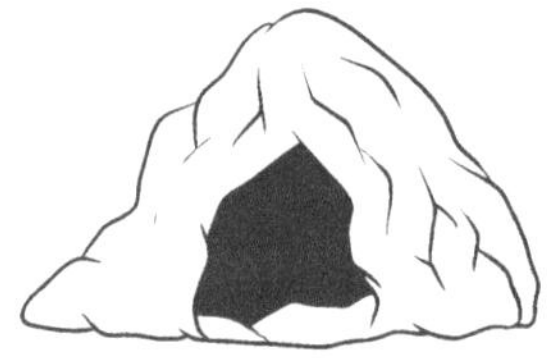

cave

e

short ĕ

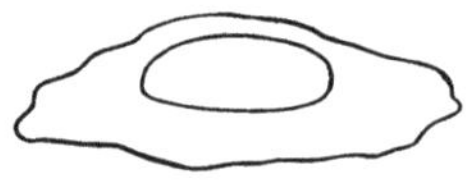

egg

long ē

leaf

i

short ĭ

milk

long ī

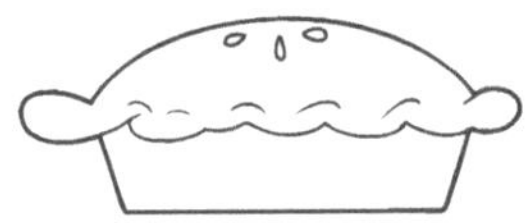

pie

o

short ŏ

top

long ō

globe

u

short ŭ

nut

long ū

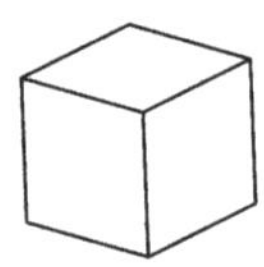

cube

Short and Long Vowels (cont.)

Say the name of the object out loud.
Draw a line from the object to the matching word.

1

leaf well

2

jam tape

3

fish pie

4

cube tub

5

coat dog

6

cave fan

7

net tree

8

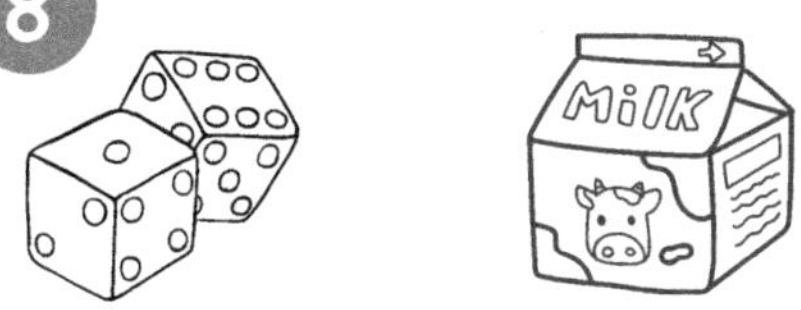

milk dice

9

lock phone

Circle all the words with a short vowel. red
Circle all the words with a long vowel. blue

Short Vowel Practice: a

1 Say the name of the object out loud.
Fill in the missing **short vowel** to make the word.

a)
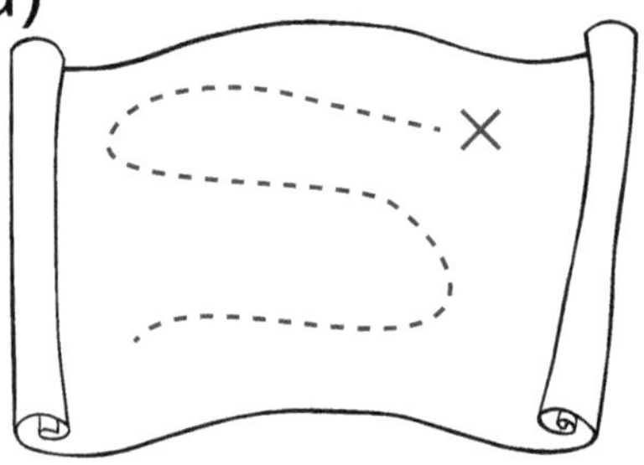
m _ p

b)

v _ n

c)

b _ t

d)

c _ p

e)

j _ m

f)

f _ n

Colour the **map**.	red	Colour the **cap**.	orange
Colour the **van**.	blue	Colour the **jam**.	purple
Colour the **bat**.	yellow	Colour the **fan**.	green

Short Vowel Practice: *a* (cont.)

2 Say the name of the object out loud.
Draw a line from the object to the matching word.

a) 

b) 

c) 

rabbit

calf

plant

3 Read the sentence.
Fill in the blank with the correct word from the box.

camel	mask

a) I saw a ____________________ in the desert.

b) For Halloween I put on a ____________________ .

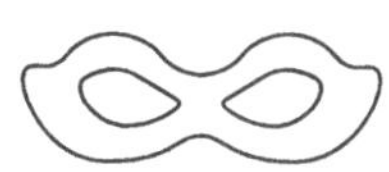

Short Vowel Practice: e

ĕ

1 Say the name of the object out loud.
Fill in the missing **short vowel** to make the word.

a)

b _ ll

b)

n _ t

c)

w _ b

d)

t _ nt

e)

j _ t

f)

w _ ll

Colour the **bell**.	orange	Colour the **tent**.	red
Colour the **net**.	brown	Colour the **jet**.	blue
Colour the **web**.	green	Colour the **well**.	yellow

Short Vowel Practice: e (cont.)

2 Say the name of the object out loud.
Draw a line from the object to the matching word.

a) 

b) 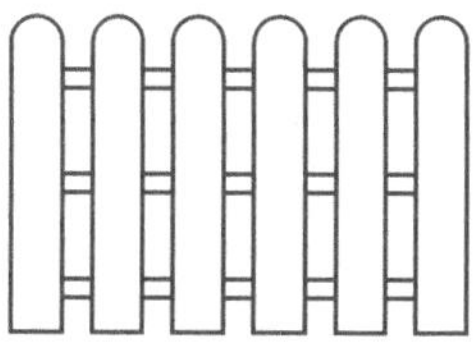

c) 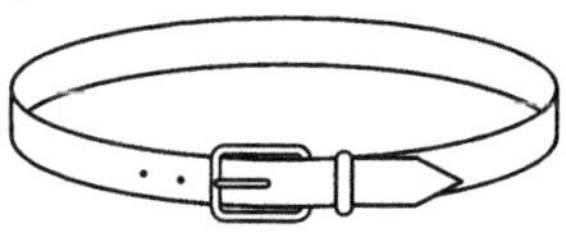

belt

fence

hen

3 Read the sentence.
Fill in the blank with the correct word from the box.

nest	steps

a) I ran down the ____________ outside. 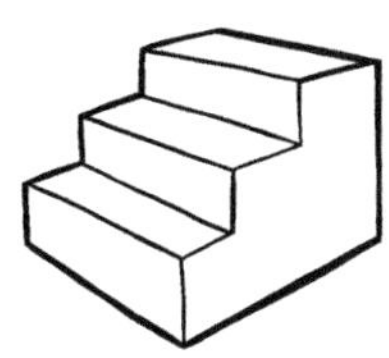

b) A bird made a ____________ in our tree. 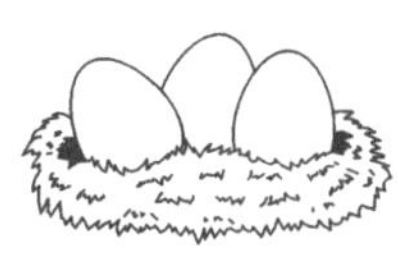

Short Vowel Practice: *i*

1 Say the name of the object out loud.
Fill in the missing **short vowel** to make the word.

a)

m ___ lk

b)

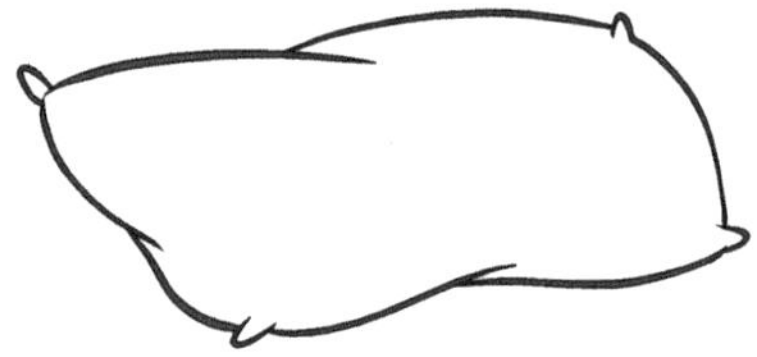

p ___ llow

c)

s ___ x

d)

f ___ sh

e)

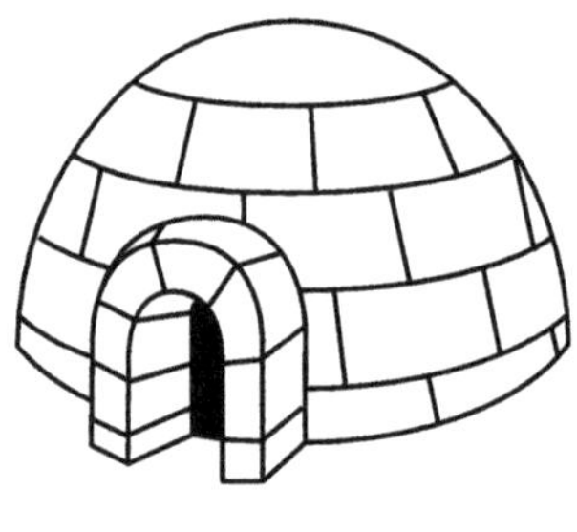

___ gloo

f)

p ___ g

Colour the **milk**.	blue	Colour the **fish**.	red
Colour the **pillow**.	yellow	Colour the **igloo**.	grey
Colour the **six**.	green	Colour the **pig**.	pink

Short Vowel Practice: *i* (cont.)

2 Say the name of the object out loud.
Draw a line from the object to the matching word.

a) 	kid
b) 	ribbon
c) 	dinner

3 Read the sentence.
Fill in the blank with the correct word from the word box.

bin	dig

a) I use a shovel to ____________ a hole.

b) I throw my recycling in a ____________ .

Short Vowel Practice: o

1 Say the name of the object out loud.
Fill in the missing **short vowel** to make the word.

a)

f x

b)

d ll

c)

m th

d)

p t

e)

l ck

f)

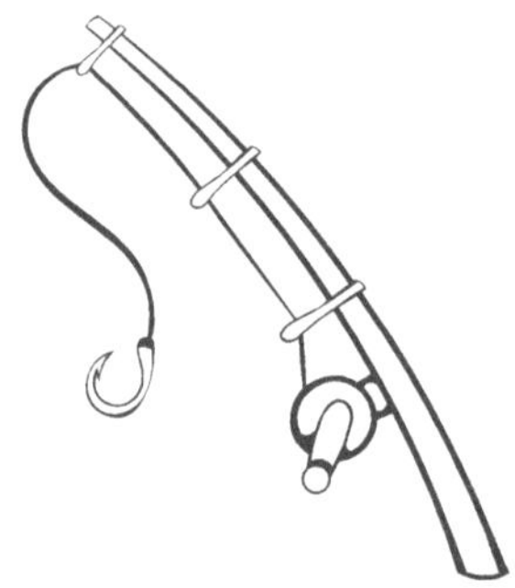

r d

Colour the **fox**.	red	Colour the **pot**.	yellow
Colour the **doll**.	blue	Colour the **lock**.	green
Colour the **moth**.	brown	Colour the **rod**.	orange

Short Vowel Practice: o (cont.)

2 Say the name of the object out loud.
Draw a line from the object to the matching word.

a) 

b) 

c) 

top

frog

log

3 Read the sentence.
Fill in the blank with the correct word from the box.

box	otter

a) At the zoo I saw an ____________________.

b) I packed all my things into a ____________________.

Short Vowel Practice: *u*

ŭ

1 Say the name of the object out loud.
Fill in the missing **short vowel** to make the word.

a)

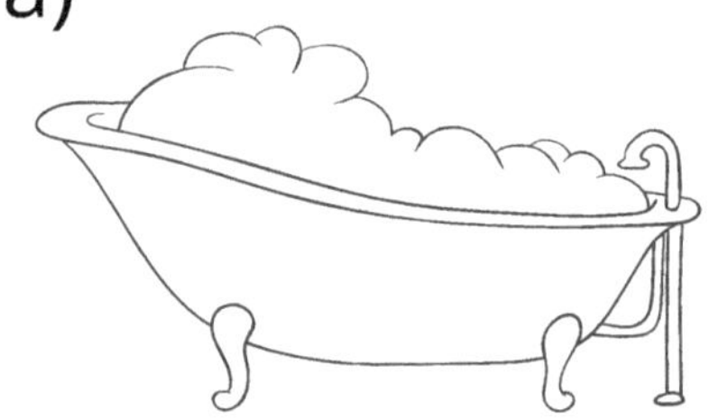

t ___ b

b)

dr ___ m

c)

n ___ t

d)

tr ___ ck

e)

l ___ nch

f)

m ___ g

Colour the **tub**.	blue	Colour the **truck**.	red
Colour the **drum**.	orange	Colour the **lunch**.	green
Colour the **nut**.	brown	Colour the **mug**.	yellow

Short Vowel Practice: *u* (cont.)

2 Say the name of the object out loud.
Draw a line from the object to the matching word.

a) 	button
b) 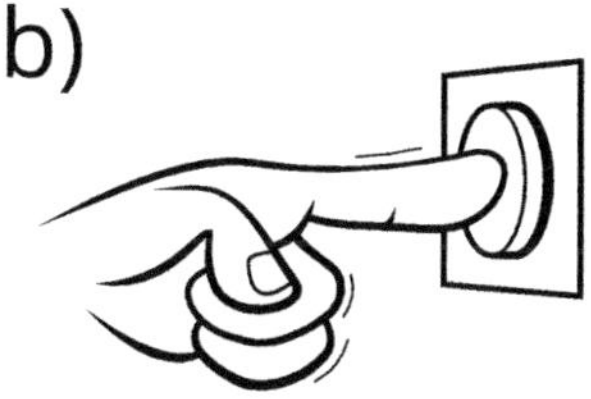	bug
c) 	sucker

3 Read the sentence.
Fill in the blank with the correct word from the box.

bus	jug

a) I took the ______________ to school today. 

b) Lucy filled a ______________ with apple juice. 

Long Vowel Practice: a

1 Say the name of the object out loud.
Fill in the missing **long vowel** to make the word.

ā

a) 

g ___ te

b) 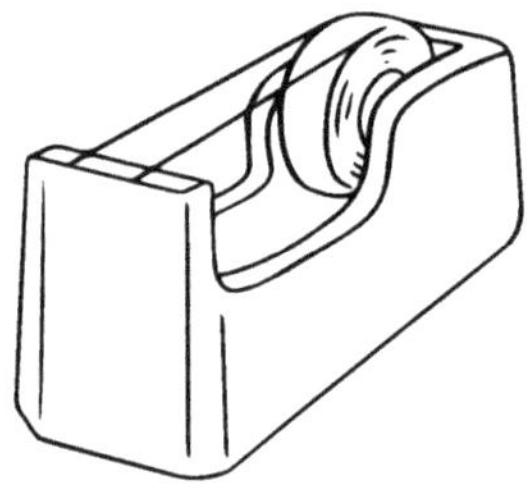

t ___ pe

c) 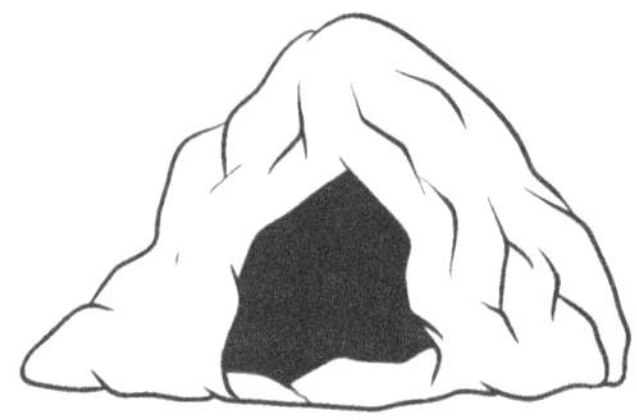

c ___ ve

d) 

pl ___ ne

e) 

g ___ me

f) 

m ___ ne

Colour the **gate**. grey

Colour the **tape**. blue

Colour the **cave**. brown

Colour the **plane**. red

Colour the **game**. yellow

Colour the **mane**. green

Long Vowel Practice: a (cont.)

2. Read the words in the box out loud.
Read the sentence.
Fill in the blank with the correct word from the box.

ape	cage	grapes	rake	snake

a) ____________ are a yummy snack.

b) The ____________ is for Timmy's pet bird.

c) My sister wants to hold a ____________ .

d) Use a ____________ to clean up leaves.

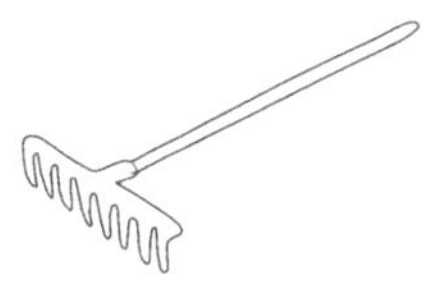

e) At the zoo I saw a big ____________ .

Long Vowel Practice: e

ē

1 Say the name of the object out loud.
Fill in the missing **long vowel** to make the word.

a)

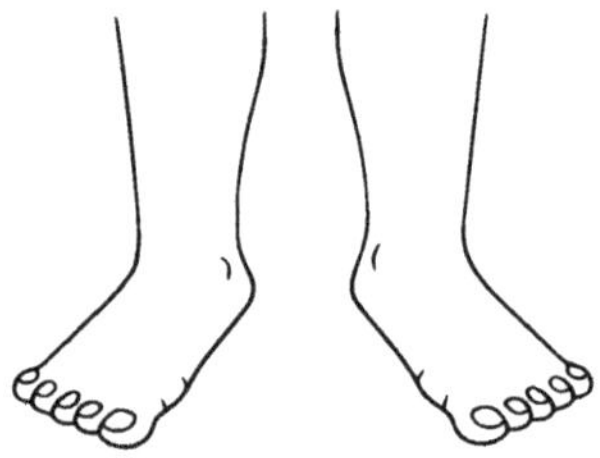

f et

b)

m al

c)

b e

d)

s al

e)

d er

f)

st am

Colour the **feet**.	blue	Colour the **seal**.	grey
Colour the **meal**.	yellow	Colour the **deer**.	brown
Colour the **bee**.	orange	Colour the **steam**.	red

Long Vowel Practice: e (cont.)

2 Read the words in the box out loud.
Read the sentence.
Fill in the blank with the correct word from the box.

cheese	jeans	key	leaf	tree

a) I bought new ________________ at the mall.

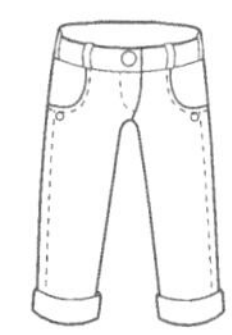

b) Amira found a pretty ________________ on her walk.

c) Ian likes to eat ________________ on his sandwich.

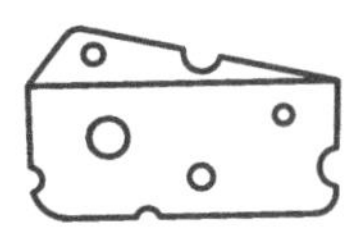

d) Julie uses a ________________ to unlock her bike.

e) We planted a ________________ in the backyard.

Long Vowel Practice: *i*

1 Say the name of the object out loud.
Fill in the missing **long vowel** to make the word.

a)

b _ ke

b)

h _ ve

c)

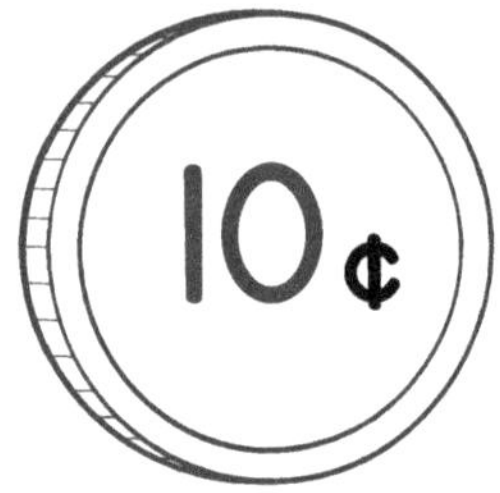

d _ me

d)

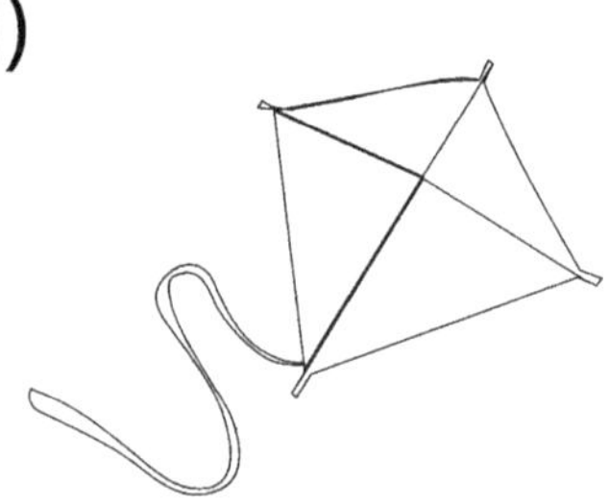

k _ te

e)

n _ ne

f)

d _ ce

Colour the **bike**.	blue	Colour the **kite**.	red
Colour the **hive**.	yellow	Colour the **nine**.	green
Colour the **dime**.	grey	Colour the **dice**.	purple

Long Vowel Practice: *i* (cont.)

2 Read the words in the box out loud.
Read the sentence.
Fill in the blank with the correct word from the box.

fire	lion	pie	slide	tire

a) We saw a ______________ at the zoo.

b) We had a ______________ while camping.

c) My grandma made a ______________ for dessert.

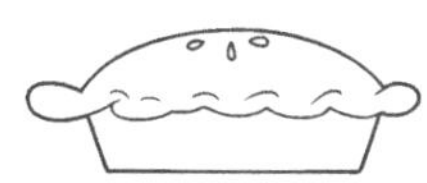

d) I like playing on the ______________ at the park.

e) My dad changed the ______________ on his car.

Long Vowel Practice: o

1 Say the name of the object out loud.
Fill in the missing **long vowel** to make the word.

ō

a)

b _ wl

b)

st _ ve

c)

r _ se

d)

n _ te

e)

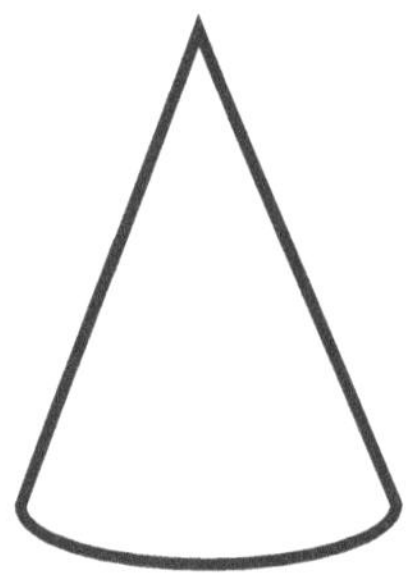

c _ ne

f)

g _ at

Colour the **bowl**. yellow
Colour the **stove**. blue
Colour the **rose**. red

Colour the **note**. green
Colour the **cone**. orange
Colour the **goat**. brown

Long Vowel Practice: o (cont.)

2 Read the words in the box out loud.
Read the sentence.
Fill in the blank with the correct word from the box.

boat	home	phone	rope	snow

a)

In the winter we get a lot of ____________ .

b)

My mom called me on the ____________ .

c)

After school Mary walks ____________ .

d)

We take our ____________ out on the lake.

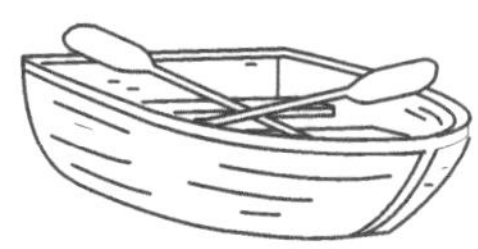

e)

I use a ____________ to tie a knot.

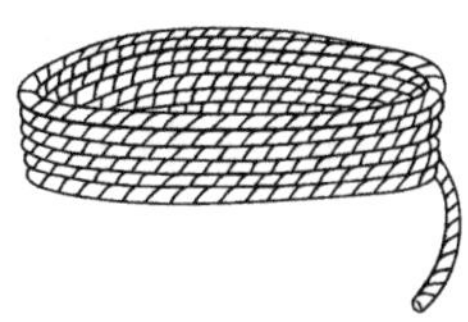

Long Vowel Practice: u

ū

1 Say the name of the object out loud.
Fill in the missing **long vowel** to make the word.

a)
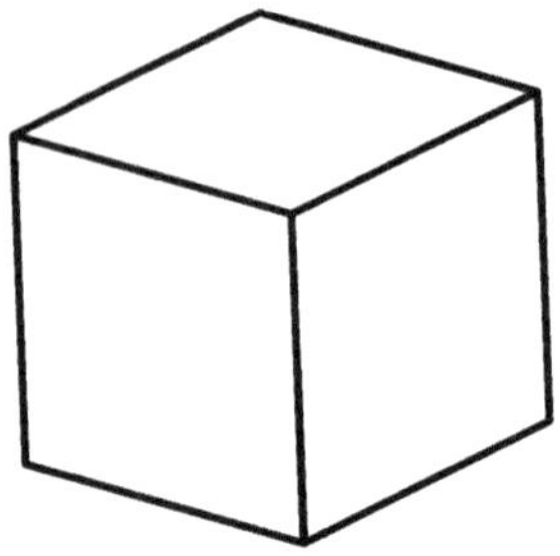
c   be

b)

m   sic

c)
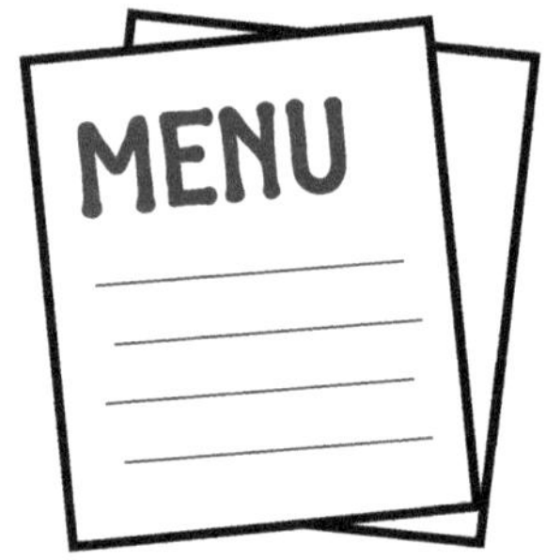

men

d)

J   ne

e)

m   le

f)

h   man

Colour the **cube**.	blue	Colour **June**.	yellow
Colour the **music**.	green	Colour the **mule**.	brown
Colour the **menu**.	red	Colour the **human**.	purple

Long Vowel Practice: *u* (cont.)

2 Read the words in the box out loud.
Read the sentence.
Fill in the blank with the correct word from the box.

cute	fuel	music	statue	tissue

a) Use a ______________ when you sneeze.

b) Dad filled the car up with ______________ .

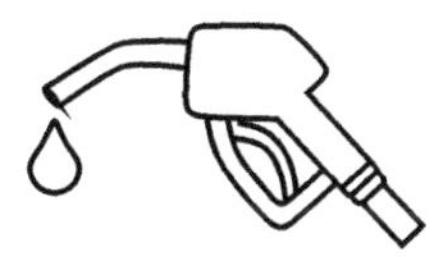

c) In the park there is a stone ______________ .

d) Tyrone listens to ______________ on his walk.

e) Hailey's new puppy is very ______________ .

Y as a Long *i* Sound

Sometimes the letter *y* makes a long *i* sound.

fly

spy

cry

sky

Y as a Long *e* Sound

Sometimes the letter *y* makes a long *e* sound.

honey

cherry

city

puppy

Y as Long Vowel Sounds

1 Say the name of the object out loud.
Circle the sound the letter ***y*** makes in the word.

a)

Long ē
Long ī

b)

Long ē
Long ī

c)

Long ē
Long ī

d)

Long ē
Long ī

e)

Long ē
Long ī

f)

Long ē
Long ī

g)

Long ē
Long ī

h)

Long ē
Long ī

i)

Long ē
Long ī

Colour the y as long *i* words.

Colour the y as long *e* words.

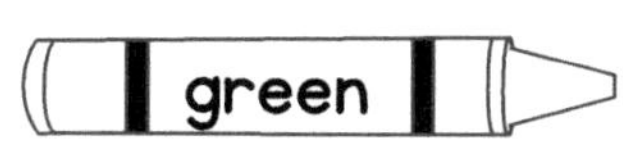

Unit 7

Words with *ai* and *ay*

1 Sort the words into the correct column.

drain	main	say	today

ai words	*ay* words

2 Say the name of the object out loud.
Draw a line from the object to the matching word.

a) 

b) 

c) 

train

spray

pail

Words with *ai* and *ay* (cont.)

3 Read the words in the box out loud.
Read the sentence.
Fill in the blank with the correct word from the box.

hay	May	nail	paint	pay

a) The farmer makes a pile of ______________.

b) There is a ______________ in the toolbox.

c) Julia's birthday is in ______________.

d) I got to ______________ my room green.

e) Mom has to ______________ for the items.

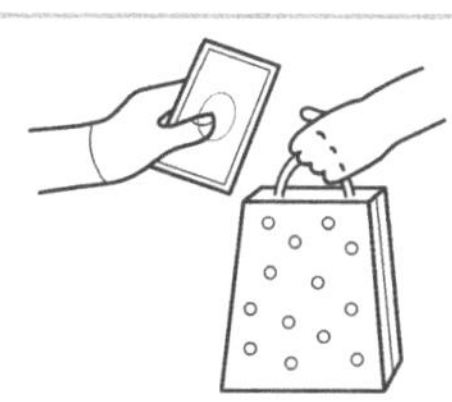

Unit 8 Words with *ee* and *ea*

1 Sort the words into the correct column.

beak	beef	cream	peel

ee words	*ea* words

2 Say the name of the object out loud.
Draw a line from the object to the matching word.

a) 

b) 

c) 

beach

leaf

sheep

Words with *ee* and *ea* (cont.)

3 Read the words in the box out loud.
Read the sentence.
Fill in the blank with the correct word from the box.

cheese	feet	seal	seeds	tea

a) Pia planted ____________ in the dirt.

b) Morgan buys socks for her ____________ .

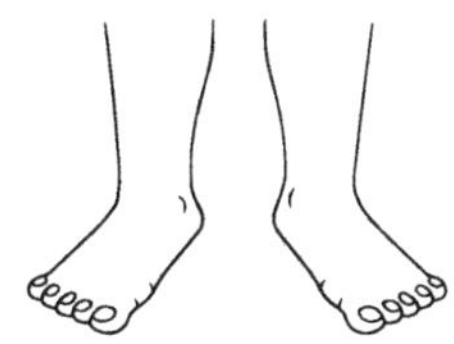

c) A ____________ jumped into the water.

d) My dad drinks ____________ every morning.

e) ____________ is my favourite pizza topping.

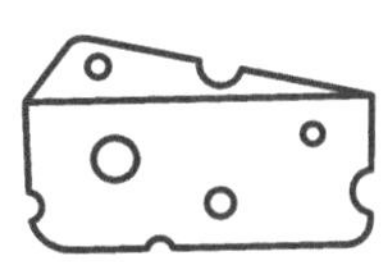

Unit 9

Words with *ie* and *igh*

1 Sort the words into the correct column.

cried	dried	high
lie	might	night

ie words	*igh* words

2 Say the name of the object out loud.
Draw a line from the object to the matching word.

a) 

b) 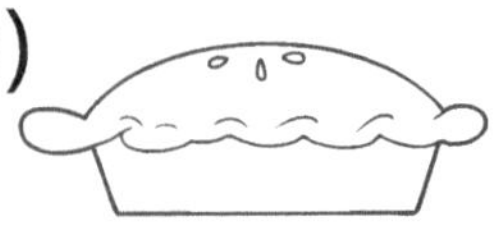

pie

light

Words with *ie* and *igh* (cont.)

3 Read the words in the box out loud.
Read the sentence.
Fill in the blank with the correct word from the box.

bright	die	knight	pie	tie

a) My dad wears a ____________ for work.

b) The ____________ goes on an adventure.

c) Roll the ____________ to play the game.

d) The sun is very ____________ .

e) My mom made ____________ for dessert.

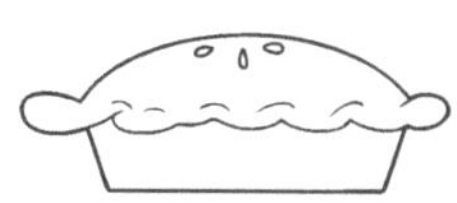

Unit 10

Words with *oa* and *ow*

1 Sort the words into the correct column.

goal grow loaf slow

oa words	*ow* words

2 Say the name of the object out loud.
Draw a line from the object to the matching word.

a) 

b) 

c) 

crow

boat

snow

Words with *oa* and *ow* (cont.)

3 Read the words in the box out loud.
Read the sentence.
Fill in the blank with the correct word from the box.

bow	bowl	coat	soap	toad

a) My new ____________ is red.

b) The ____________ caught a fly.

c) The ____________ is for my soup.

d) Use ____________ to wash your hands.

e) Put the ____________ on the present.

Unit 11 Words with *oo* and *u*

1 Say the name of the object out loud.
Draw a line from the object to the matching word.

a) 

b) 

c) 

glue

pool

suit

2 Read the sentence.
Fill in the blank with the correct word from the box.

flute	moon	tooth

a) The ____________ is so bright in the dark sky. 

b) Alexa knows how to play the ____________ . 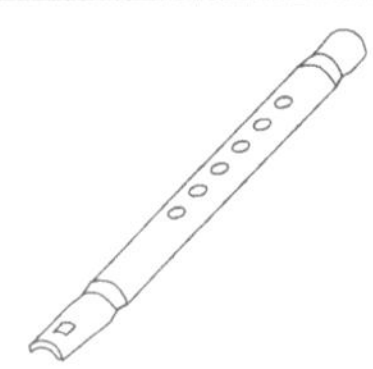

c) My little brother's ____________ fell out! 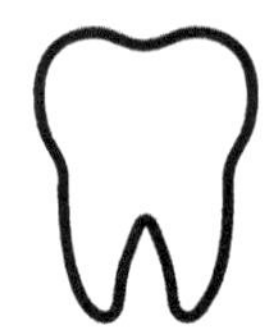

Unit 12

Words with *ew*, *ue*, and *ui*

1 Sort the words into the correct column.

blue clue flew fruit stew suit

ew words	*ue* words	*ui* words

2 Say the name of the object out loud.
Draw a line from the object to the matching word.

a) 

b) 

c) 

glue

fruit

jewel

Unit 13 Words with *oi* and *oy*

1 Sort the words into the correct column.

annoy **enjoy** **join** **point**

oi words	*oy* words

2 Say the name of the object out loud.
Draw a line from the object to the matching word.

a) 

b) 

c) 

soil

cowboy

toilet

Words with *oi* and *oy* (cont.)

3 Read the words in the box out loud.
Read the sentence.
Fill in the blank with the correct word from the box.

boil	boy	coin	noise	toy

a) There is a new ______________ at our school.

b) Mom bought me a new ______________ .

c) Charlie found a ______________ on the ground.

d) You have to ______________ the water for pasta.

e) There is too much ______________ in here.

Unit 14 Words with *ow* and *ou*

1 Sort the words into the correct column.

count	hour	howl	town

ow words	*ou* words

2 Say the name of the object out loud.
Draw a line from the object to the matching word.

a) 

b) 

c) 

crown

house

mouse

Words with *ow* and *ou* (cont.)

3. Read the words in the box out loud.
Read the sentence.
Fill in the blank with the correct word from the box.

cloud	clown	cow	flour	flower

a) The ______________ smells sweet.

b) There is a ______________ in the field.

c) A fluffy ______________ is in the sky.

d) A ______________ was at the circus.

e) Put the ______________ in the mixing bowl.

Unit 15 Words with *-le*

1 Use the words in the box to write the correct *-le* word next to the picture.

apple	candle	noodle
puddle	table	turtle

a)  ____________

b)  ____________

c)  ____________

d)  ____________

e)  ____________

f)  ____________

2 Write the **final consonant and *-le*** to complete the word.

a) 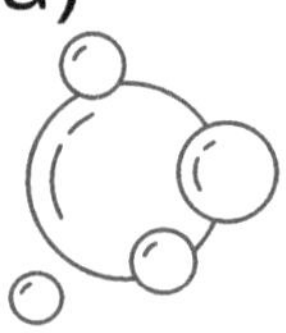 bub ____________

b)  waf ____________

c)  puz ____________

d)  ket ____________

Words with Silent Letters

1 Say the name of the object out loud.
Circle the **silent letter** for each word.

a)

knight

b)

wrist

c)

lamb

2 Read the sentence.
Fill in the blank with the correct word from the box.

comb	knife	write

a) Use a ________________ to fix your hair.

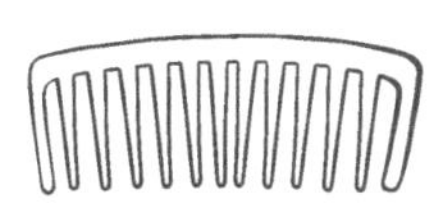

b) Jerry uses a pen to ________________ a letter.

c) The chef uses a ________________ to cut food.

Unit 17

R-Controlled Vowels

ar, *er*, *ir*, *or*, and *ur* are called *r*-controlled vowels.

1 Fill in the missing ***r*-controlled vowel** to make the word.

a)

b ___ n

b)

h ___ se

c)

tig ___

d)

b ___ d

e)

t ___ tle

f)

sh ___ k

Colour the **barn**. red
Colour the **horse**. brown
Colour the **tiger**. orange
Colour the **bird**. yellow
Colour the **turtle**. green
Colour the **shark**. blue

R-Controlled Vowels (cont.)

ar, ***er***, ***ir***, ***or***, and ***ur*** are called ***r***-controlled vowels.

2 Fill in the missing ***r*-controlled vowel** to make the word.

a)

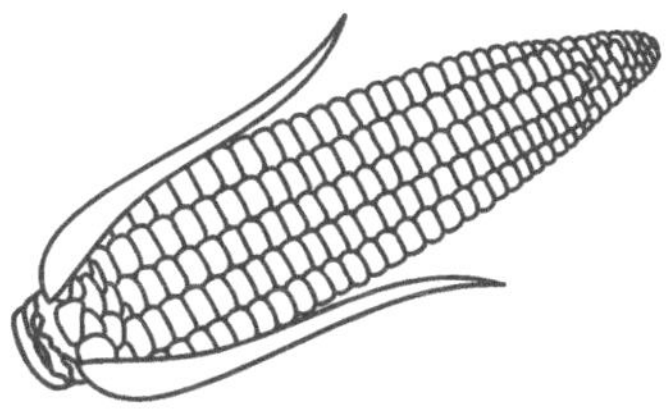

c ____ n

b)

sh ____ t

c)

wat ____

d)

sc ____ f

e)

p ____ se

f)

h ____ n

Colour the **corn**. yellow
Colour the **shirt**. red
Colour the **water**. blue
Colour the **scarf**. purple
Colour the **purse**. green
Colour the **horn**. orange

R-Controlled Vowels (cont.)

***ar*, *er*, *ir*, *or*, and *ur* are called *r-controlled vowels*.**

3 Fill in the missing ***r*-controlled vowel** to make the word.

a)

flow ____

b)

p ____ k

c)

t ____ n

d)

sk ____ t

e)

n ____ se

f)

st ____ m

Colour the **flower**.	yellow	Colour the **skirt**.	green
Colour the **park**.	blue	Colour the **nurse**.	pink
Colour the **turn**.	red	Colour the **storm**.	grey

R-Controlled Vowels (cont.)

ar, *er*, *ir*, *or*, and *ur* are called *r-controlled vowels*.

4 Fill in the missing ***r*-controlled vowel** to make the word.

a) 

ott___

b) 

d___t

c) 

f___k

d) 

st___

e) 

s___f

f) 

pap___

Colour the **otter**. purple
Colour the **dirt**. brown
Colour the **fork**. red
Colour the **star**. yellow
Colour the **surf**. blue
Colour the **paper**. orange

Unit 18

Word Families: *all* and *ell*

1 Sort the words into the correct column.

call	cell	fall
fell	hall	spell

all words	*ell* words

2 Circle the ***all*** words. 

Circle the ***ell*** words. 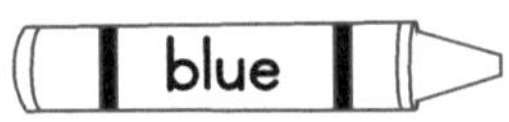

a) Tell Sarah to kick the ball.

b) My mom said not to yell at the mall.

Word Families: *all* and *ell* (cont.)

3 Draw a line from the object to the matching word.

a) 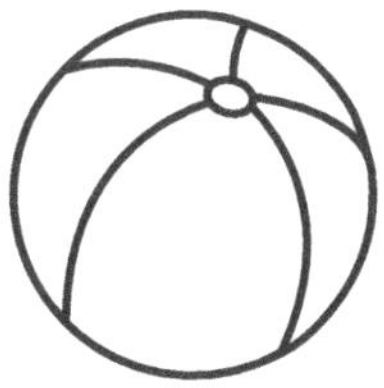

b) 

c) 

well

bell

ball

4 Read the sentence.
Fill in the blank with the correct word from the box.

small	smell

a) The flower has a nice ________________ .

b) My new kitten is very ________________ .

Word Families: *at* and *an*

1 Sort the words into the correct column.

bat	can	man
mat	pat	ran

at words	*an* words

2 Circle the ***at*** words. 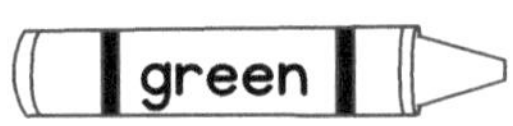

Circle the ***an*** words. 

a) That silly cat ran right by me!

b) The little puppy sat by the man.

Word Families: *at* and *an* (cont.)

3. Draw a line from the object to the matching word.

a) 		pan
b) 		rat
c) 		hat

4. Read the sentence.
Fill in the blank with the correct word from the box.

fan	fat

a) Turn on the ____________ to cool down.

b) The cow at the barn was very ____________.

Unit 20

Word Families: *op* and *ap*

1 Sort the words into the correct column.

drop	hop	lap
nap	pop	zap

op words	*ap* words

2 Circle the ***op*** words. 

Circle the ***ap*** words. 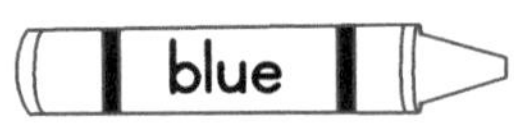

a) The bucket of sap is filled to the top.

b) At the end of the day, the cop took a nap.

Word Families: *op* and *ap* (cont.)

3 Draw a line from the object to the matching word.

a) 	clap
b) 	top
c) 	shop

4 Read the sentence.
Fill in the blank with the correct word from the box.

map	mop

a) I clean the floor with a ________________ . 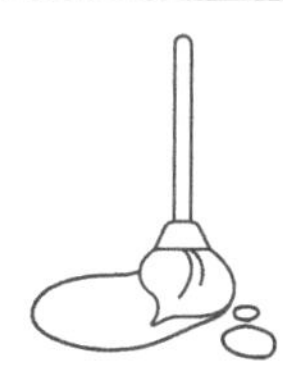

b) The treasure is marked on the ________________ . 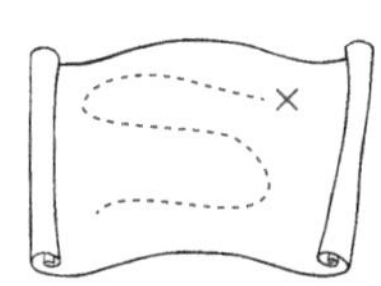

Word Families: *ut* and *ug*

1 Sort the words into the correct column.

bug	cut	gut
hug	jug	rut

ut words	*ug* words

2 Circle the ***ut*** words. 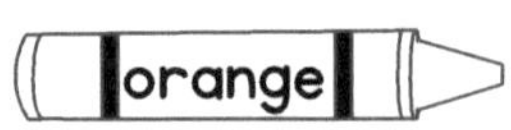

Circle the ***ug*** words. 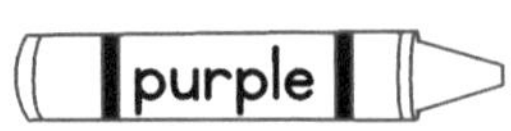

a) A bug landed on me but then it flew away.

b) I dug a hole and got a small cut.

Word Families: *ut* and *ug* (cont.)

3 Draw a line from the object to the matching word.

a) 

b) 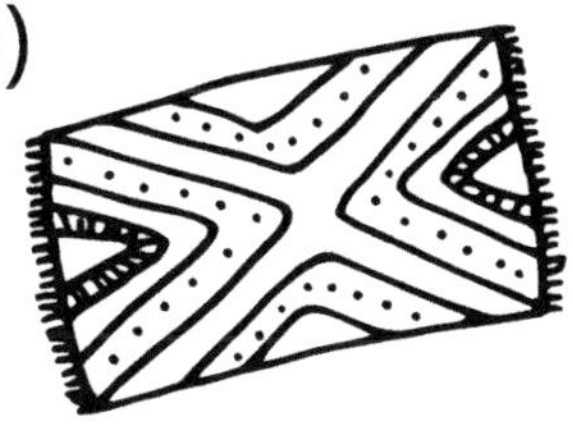

c) 

rug

mug

nut

4 Read the sentence.
Fill in the blank with the correct word from the word box.

hug	hut

a) Tracy gave her new cat a ______________ .

b) Mason went camping in a ______________ .

Unit 22

Word Families: *en* and *in*

1 Sort the words into the correct column.

den	men	spin
ten	tin	win

en words	*in* words

2 Circle the ***en*** words. blue

Circle the ***in*** words. green

a) At ten I tried to win a juggling contest.

b) The men threw the tin in the garbage.

Word Families: *en* and *in* (cont.)

3 Draw a line from the object to the matching word.

a) 

b) 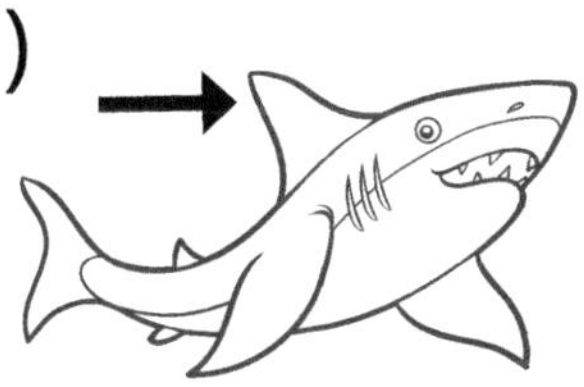

c) 

bin

hen

fin

4 Read the sentence.
Fill in the blank with the correct word from the box.

pen	pin

a) The ______________ is sharp. 

b) Use a ______________ to write a letter. 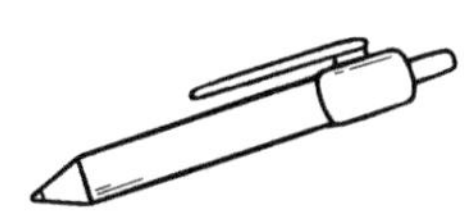

Unit 23

Word Families Review

1 Draw a line from the object to the matching word.

a) 

b) 

c) 

d) 

e) 

bell

shop

hat

mug

pin

Colour the **hat**.	red	Colour the **shop**.	green
Colour the **bell**.	orange	Colour the **mug**.	purple
Colour the **pin**.	blue		

Word Families Review (cont.)

2 Choose the correct word to fill in the blank.

a) My sister turns ______________ years old today. tin / ten

b) I filled the ______________ with juice. jug / jut

c) Turn on the ______________ to wash your hands. top / tap

d) Mom cooks the chicken in a ______________ . pan / pat

e) We hang the picture on the ______________ . well / wall

Unit 24

Words with *nd* and *nt*

1. Sort the words into the correct column.

bent	land	mend
pant	send	want

nd words	*nt* words

2. Circle the ***nd*** words. green

Circle the ***nt*** words. red

a) I went to see my kind cousin yesterday.

b) My favourite band sent me a letter!

Words with *nd* and *nt* (cont.)

3 Say the word. Then, trace the word.

hand

ant

pond

wind

tent

plant

sand

wand

mint

print

Words with *ow*

1. Say the name of the object out loud. Draw a line from the object to the matching word. Circle the ***ow*** in the word.

a) 	bow
b) 	crow
c) 	rainbow
d) 	tow
e) 	snow

Colour the **snow**. blue
Colour the **tow**. yellow
Colour the **bow**. pink
Colour the **rainbow**. red
Colour the **crow**. black

Words with *ow* (cont.)

2 Say the name of the object out loud.
Circle the objects that have ***ow*** in their name.

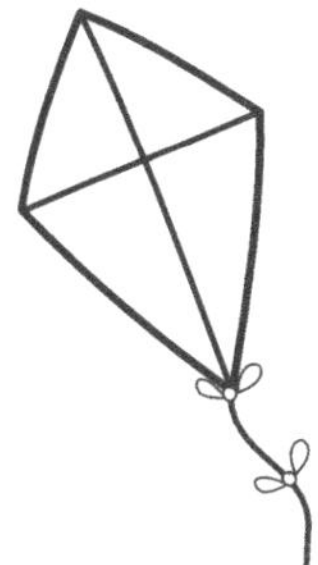

3 Read the sentence.
Fill in the blank with the correct word from the box.

down	grow

a) The weeds ________________ quickly.

b) Turn ________________ the music.

Unit 26 Words with a Short *oo* Sound

1 Say the name of the object out loud. Draw a line from the object to the matching word. Circle the ***oo*** in the word.

a) 	hook
b) 	wood
c) 	book
d) 	foot
e) 	cook

Colour the **foot**. blue

Colour the **cook**. green

Colour the **wood**. brown

Colour the **book**. red

Colour the **hook**. orange

Words with a Short *oo* Sound (cont.)

2 Fill in the blank with the best **short *oo*** word.

a) ________ at the clouds in the sky.		took look
b) This is a ________ sweater.		wool woof
c) You are a ________ friend.		book good
d) Jaime's dog likes to ________ .		woof took

3 Find all the **short *oo*** words in the word search.

Y	S	Z	B	P
X	T	O	O	K
F	O	O	T	V
H	O	O	D	Z
T	D	W	M	Q

Words to search for:

foot
hood
stood
took

Unit 27 Words with a Long oo Sound

1. Say the name of the object out loud. Draw a line from the object to the matching word. Circle the ***oo*** in the word.

a) 	boot
b) 	moon
c) 	pool
d) 	food
e) 	zoo

Colour the **pool**. blue

Colour the **zoo**. green

Colour the **moon**. brown

Colour the **boot**. red

Colour the **food**. purple

Words with a Long oo Sound (cont.)

2 Fill in the blank with the best **long *oo*** word.

a) Today I cleaned my ____________.	room moon
b) My dad has a big ____________ box.	zoo tool
c) ____________ it will be time for lunch.	too soon
d) I ate the soup with a ____________.	spoon boot

3 Find all the **long *oo*** words in the word search.

S	C	O	O	P
P	O	V	W	X
R	O	O	F	Y
Z	L	Q	N	R
X	B	O	O	M

Words to search for:

boom
cool
roof
scoop

Prefixes

A prefix is added to the beginning of a word. *Dis-* and *un-* mean ***not***.

Lia **dis**likes broccoli.

Ian is **un**afraid of the dark.

Write ***dis-*** or ***un-*** before the word.

1. Mia needs to ______tie her shoes to take them off.

2. Liam ______agrees that apples are tasty.

3. It is ______safe to ride a bike without a helmet.

4. Tony ______likes waking up early.

Suffixes

A suffix is added to the end of a word.
-ful means ***full of***. ***-less*** means ***without***.

Joy's shirt is colourful.

The hero on TV was fearless.

Write ***-ful*** or ***-less*** after the word.

1. The long line at the store felt end __________ .

2. Alicia is care __________ not to spill her drink.

3. Those bugs are harm __________ to the garden.

4. The home __________ puppy was finally adopted.

Reading Skills Checklist

Build fluency, comprehension, word detective skills, and a love for reading by providing a comfortable environment when reading with your child. Set aside time each day to read together. Take turns reading with your child.

Reading with Fluency

- ☐ Automatically read and understand some high-frequency words and words of personal interest or significance, in a variety of reading contexts
- ☐ Predict the meaning of, and solve, unfamiliar words using different types of cues, including
  - ✔ semantic (meaning) cues
  - ✔ syntactic (language structure) cues
  - ✔ graphophonic (phonological and graphic) cues
- ☐ Read appropriate, familiar texts at a sufficient rate and with sufficient expression to convey the sense of the text to the reader

Reflecting on Reading Skills and Strategies

- ☐ Begin to identify, with support and direction, a few strategies they found helpful before, during, and after reading
- ☐ Explain, initially with support and direction, how their skills in listening, speaking, writing, viewing, and representing help them make sense of what they read

How to Choose a Book for Your Child to Practise Reading

Use the five finger rule:

1. Open the book to any page and ask your child to read.
2. Put up a finger every time your child does not know a word.
3. If you have put up more than five fingers before the end of the page, this book is too hard for your child.

Sight Words to Practice

As a key part to learning to read, practise recognizing sight words with your child. The Fry word list below contains the most common words used in English listed in order of frequency and includes all parts of speech. Copy these sight words onto word cards. The goal is for your child to recognize these sight words instantly.

the	or	will	number
of	one	up	no
and	had	other	way
a	by	about	could
to	words	out	people
in	but	many	my
is	not	then	than
you	what	them	first
that	all	these	water
it	were	so	been
he	we	some	called
was	when	her	who
for	your	would	oil
on	can	make	sit
are	said	like	now
as	there	him	find
with	use	into	long
his	an	time	down
they	each	has	day
I	which	look	did
at	she	two	get
be	do	more	come
this	how	write	made
have	their	go	may
from	if	see	part

Sight Words: *the, of, and, a, to*

1 Read the sight words. Use the legend to colour the sight word.

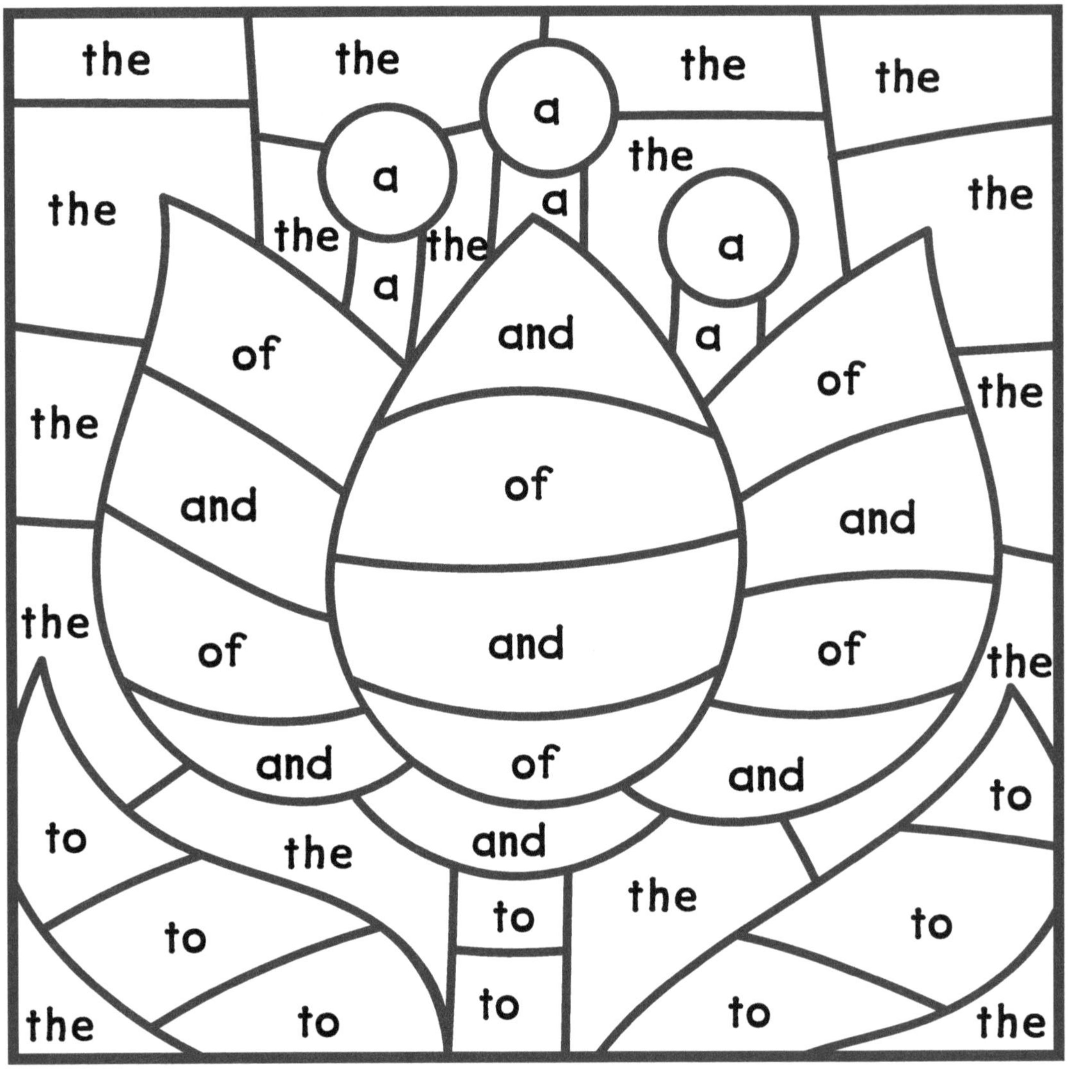

Legend

- **the** — blue
- **of** — red
- **and** — orange
- **a** — yellow
- **to** — green

2 Read the sentence. Use the legend to circle the sight words.

a) The cat is on a mat.

b) Get out of bed.

c) Max and Pat like to run.

d) I see a frog.

e) Go to the car.

Sight Words: *in, is, you, that, it*

1 Read the sight words. Use the legend to colour the sight word.

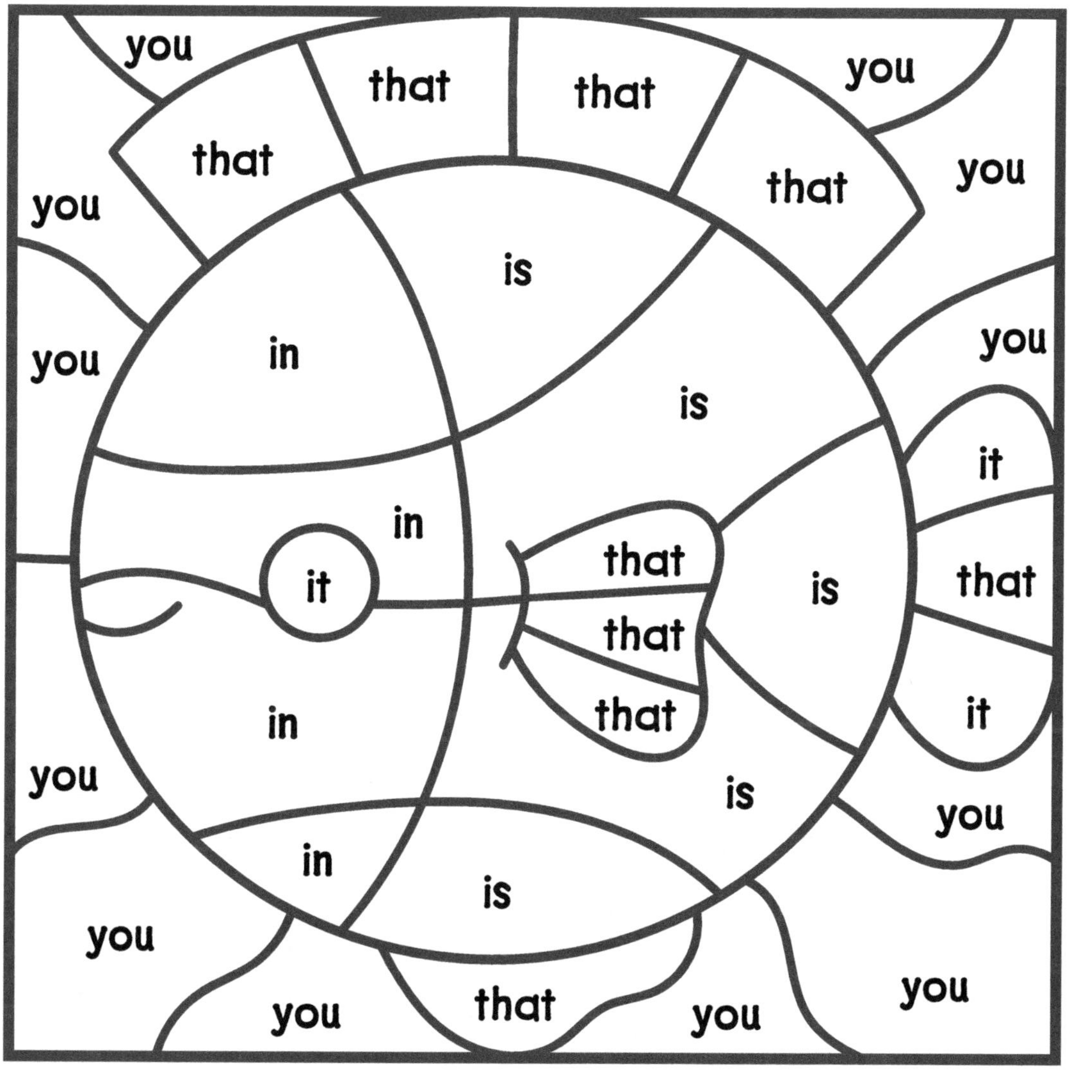

Legend

- in — yellow
- is — orange
- you — blue
- that — red
- it — black

2 Read the sentence. Use the legend to circle the sight words.

a) It is in my bag.

b) You are it!

c) That is a bird.

d) I love you.

e) She is in that class.

Sight Words: *he, was, for, on, are*

1 Read the sight words. Use the legend to colour the sight word.

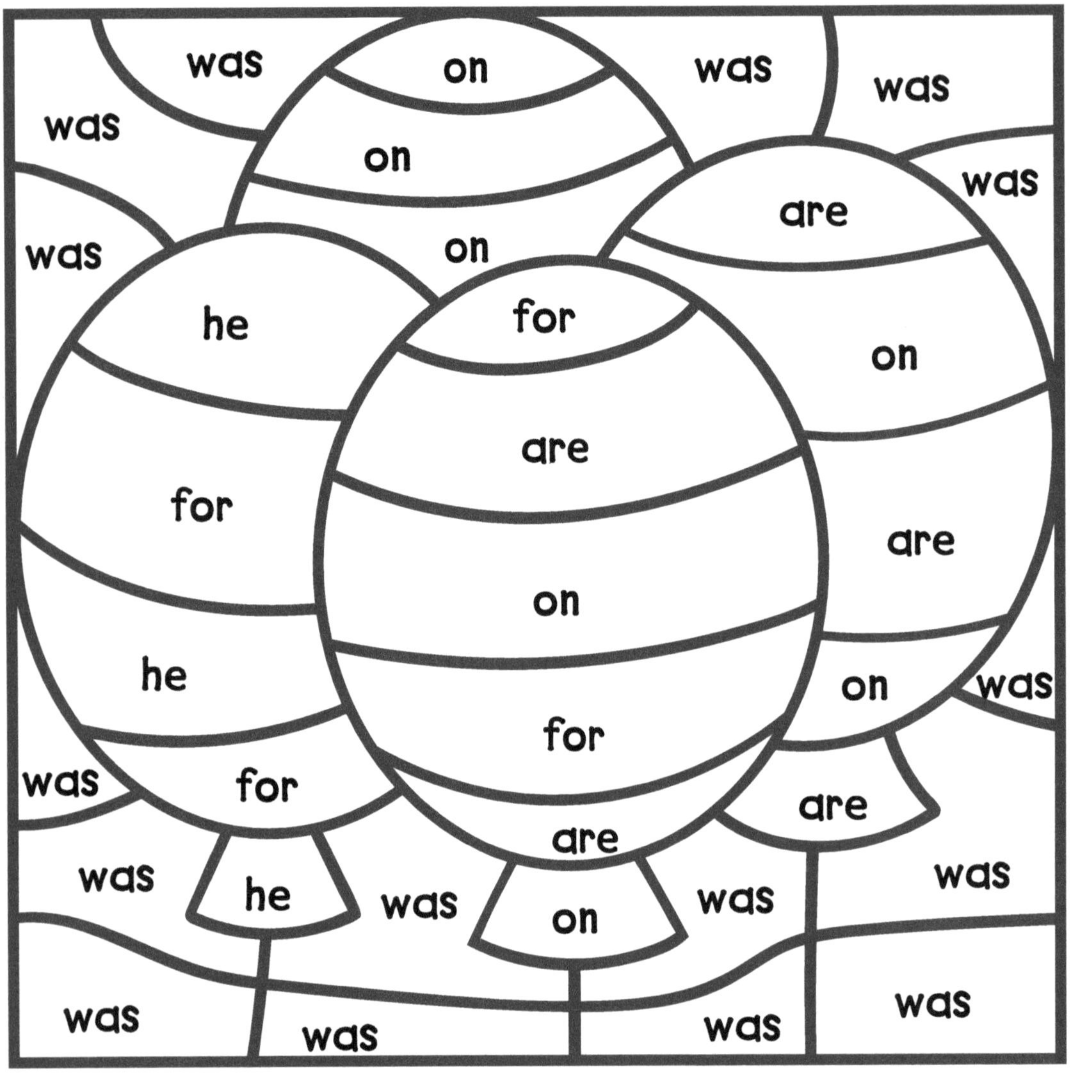

Legend

- he — purple
- was — blue
- for — green
- on — yellow
- are — red

2 Read the sentence. Use the legend to circle the sight words.

a) He is my friend.

b) How was your day?

c) This is for my mom.

d) The hat is on the box.

e) We are at home.

Sight Words: *as, with, his, they, I*

1 Read the sight words. Use the legend to colour the sight word.

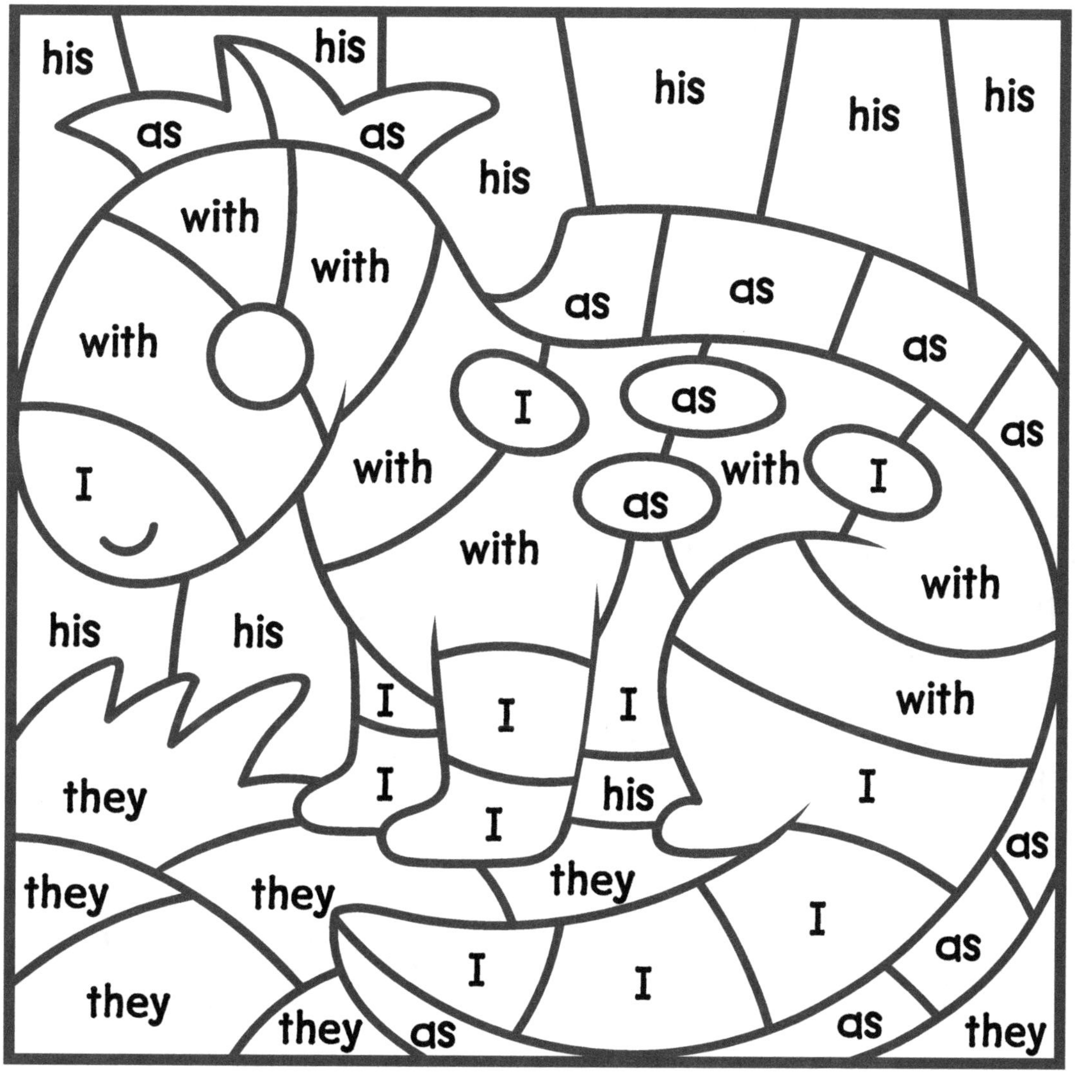

Legend

- as — blue
- with — purple
- his — orange
- they — green
- I — pink

2 Read the sentence. Use the legend to circle the sight words.

a) She is as busy as a bee.

b) Come with me.

c) His name is Sam.

d) They are at the park.

e) I can run fast.

Sight Words: *at, be, this, have, from*

1 Read the sight words. Use the legend to colour the sight word.

Legend

at	blue
be	brown
this	orange
have	green
from	purple

2 Read the sentence. Use the legend to circle the sight words.

a) I am at the zoo.

b) Will you be at the zoo?

c) This is a lion.

d) I have a map.

e) The map is from the zoo.

Sight Words: *or, one, had, by, words*

1 Read the sight words. Use the legend to colour the sight word.

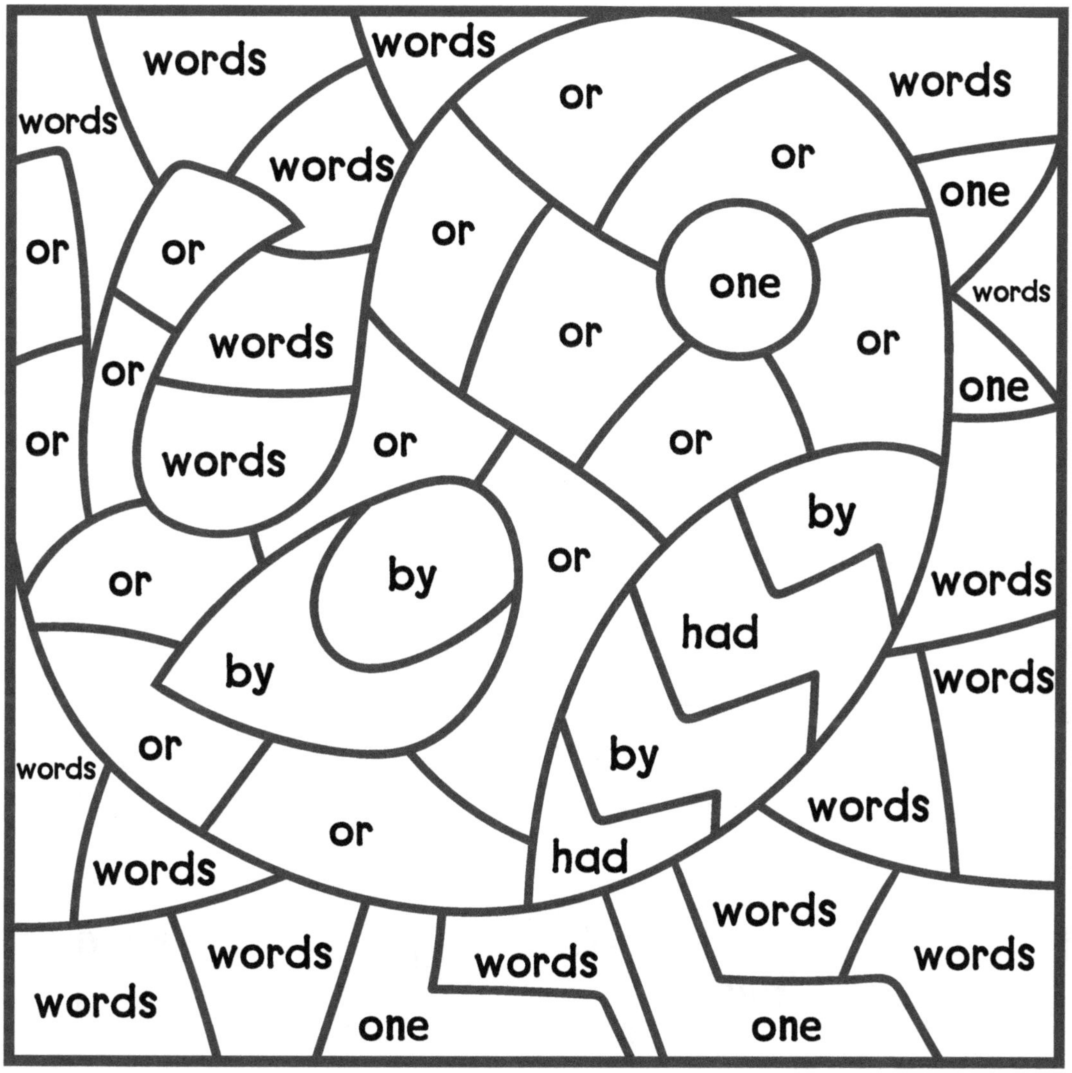

Legend

- or — purple
- one — yellow
- had — red
- by — pink
- words — blue

2 Read the sentence. Use the legend to circle the sight words.

a) Pick one apple.

b) One apple or two?

c) I had a red apple.

d) Eat the apple by the tree.

e) The words are small.

Sight Words: *but, not, what, all, were*

1 Read the sight words. Use the legend to colour the sight word.

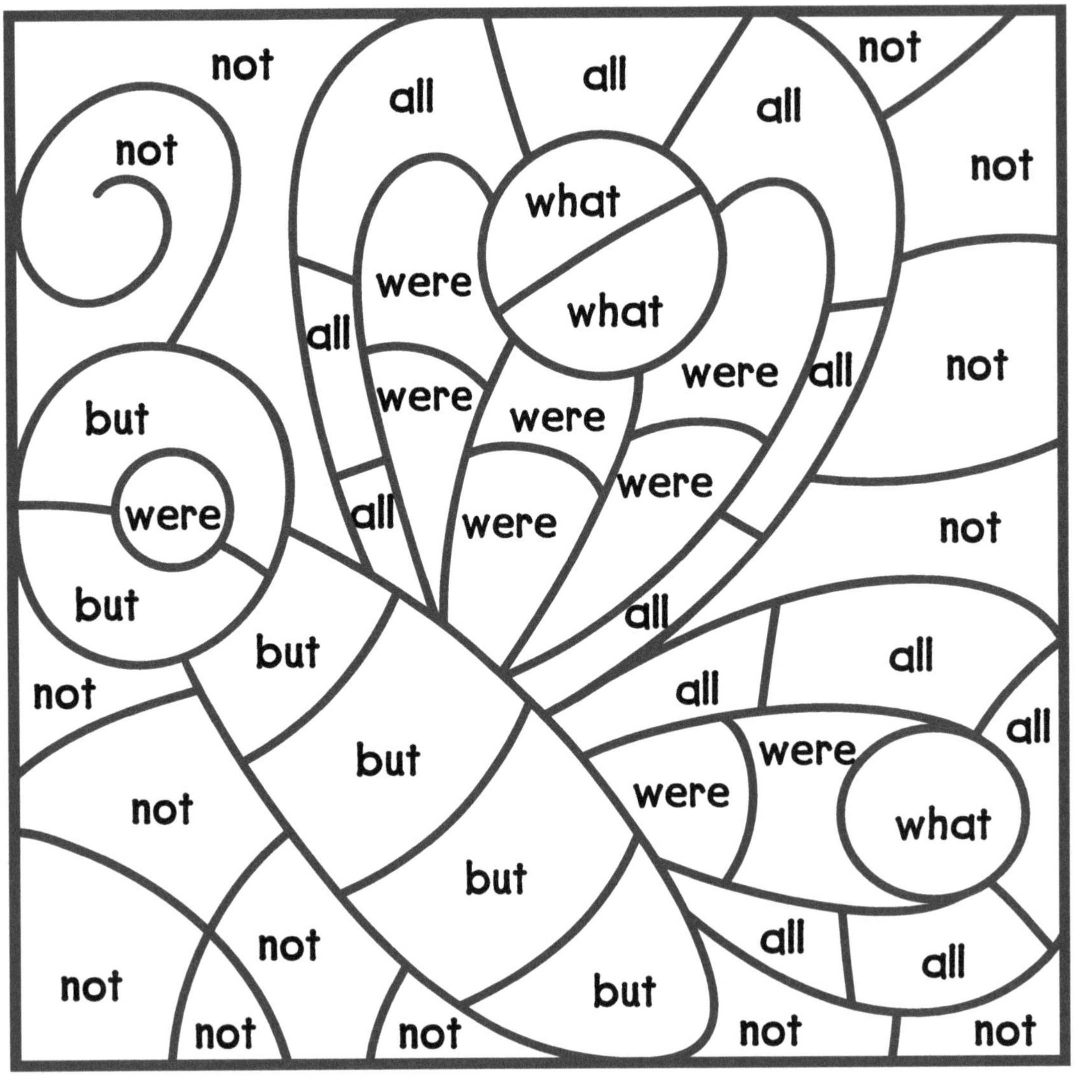

Legend

- **but** — brown
- **not** — blue
- **what** — green
- **all** — red
- **were** — yellow

2 Read the sentence. Use the legend to circle the sight words.

a) I have all four cars.

b) All the cars are fast.

c) But the cars are not big.

d) What colour were the cars?

e) They were all blue cars.

Sight Words: *we, when, your, can, said*

1 Read the sight words. Use the legend to colour the sight word.

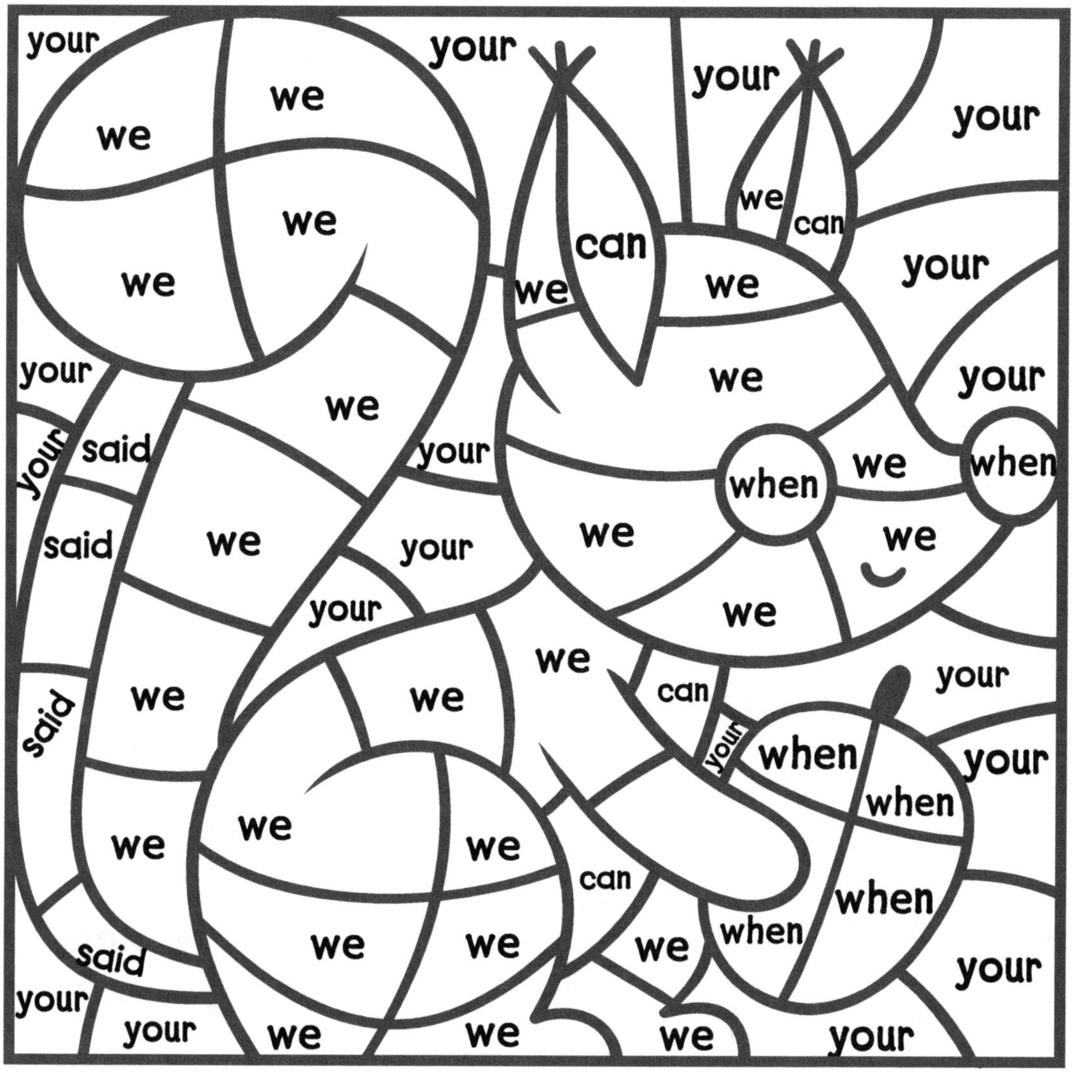

Legend

we	orange
when	brown
your	green
can	pink
said	red

2 Read the sentence. Use the legend to circle the sight words.

a) We are at the park.

b) When can we play?

c) Can your mom come, too?

d) Your ball is here.

e) She said, "yes."

Sight Words: *there, use, an, each, which*

1 Read the sight words. Use the legend to colour the sight word.

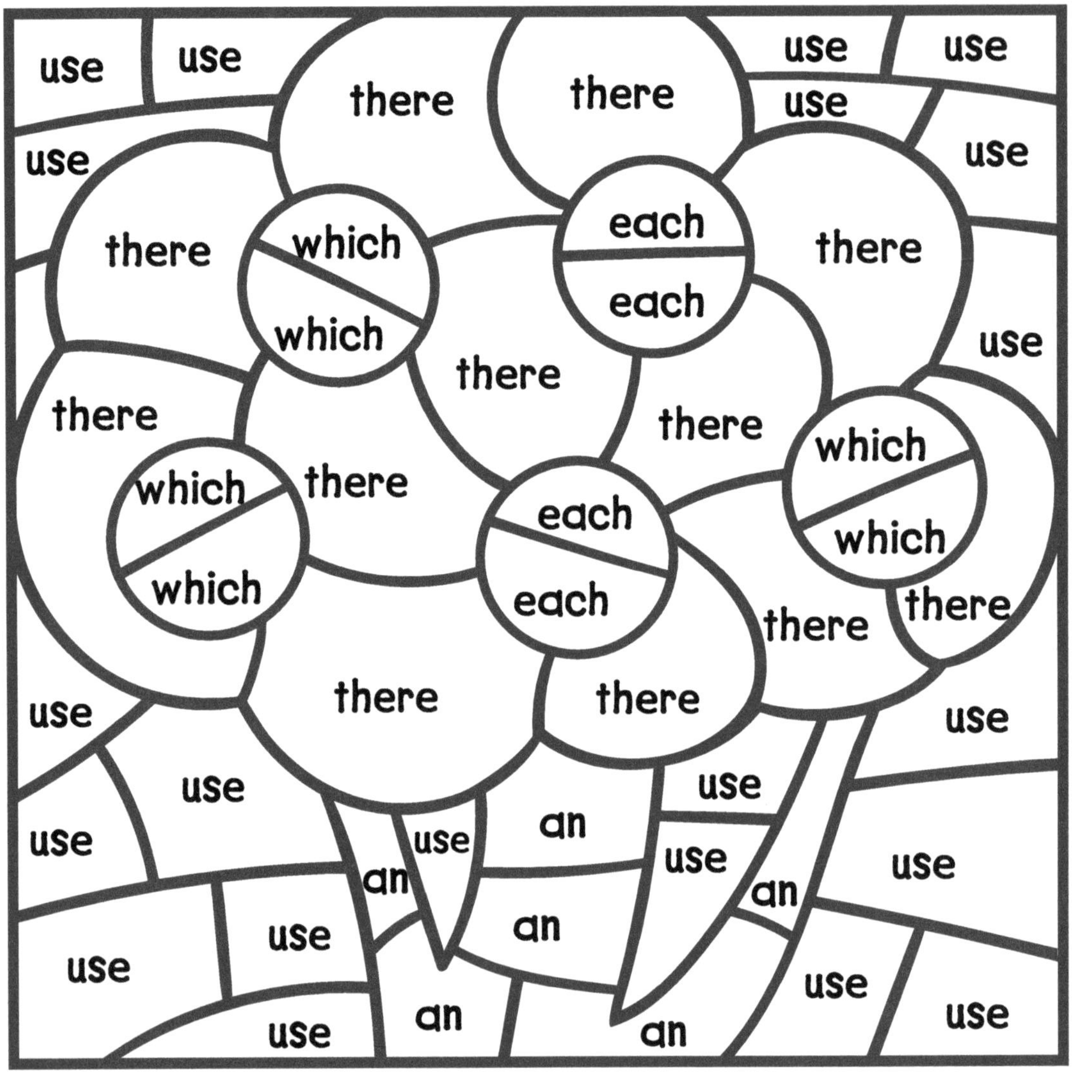

Legend

- there — green
- use — blue
- an — brown
- each — red
- which — orange

2 Read the sentence. Use the legend to circle the sight words.

a) There are five cars.

b) Use one to race.

c) Each car is fast.

d) An orange car is there.

e) Which car is yours?

Sight Words: *she, do, how, their, if*

1 Read the sight words. Use the legend to colour the sight word.

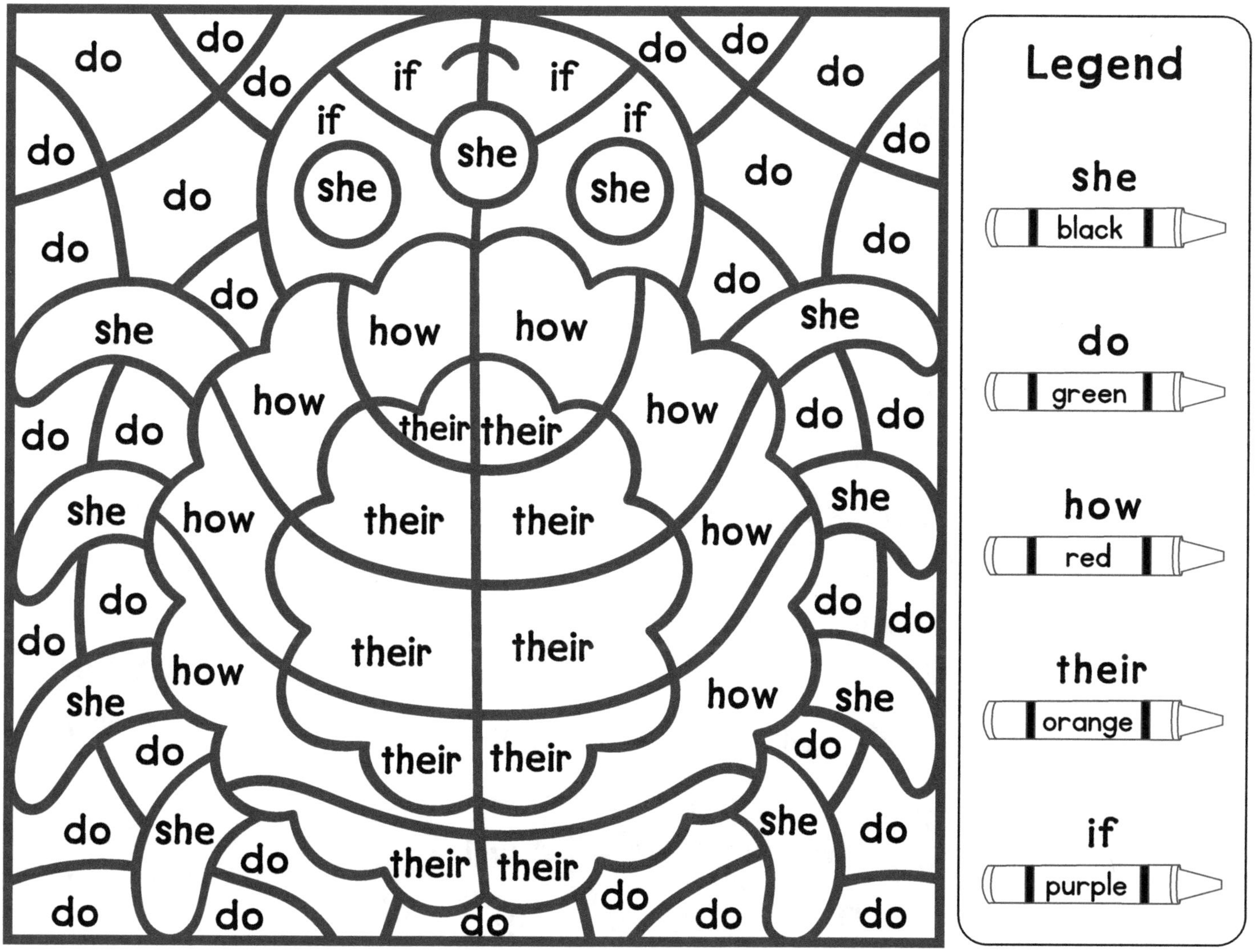

2 Read the sentence. Use the legend to circle the sight words.

a) She has a kite.

b) How does she fly it?

c) Their kites are up, too.

d) Do they know how?

e) Fly it if you can.

Sight Words: *will, up, other, about, out*

1 Read the sight words. Use the legend to colour the sight word.

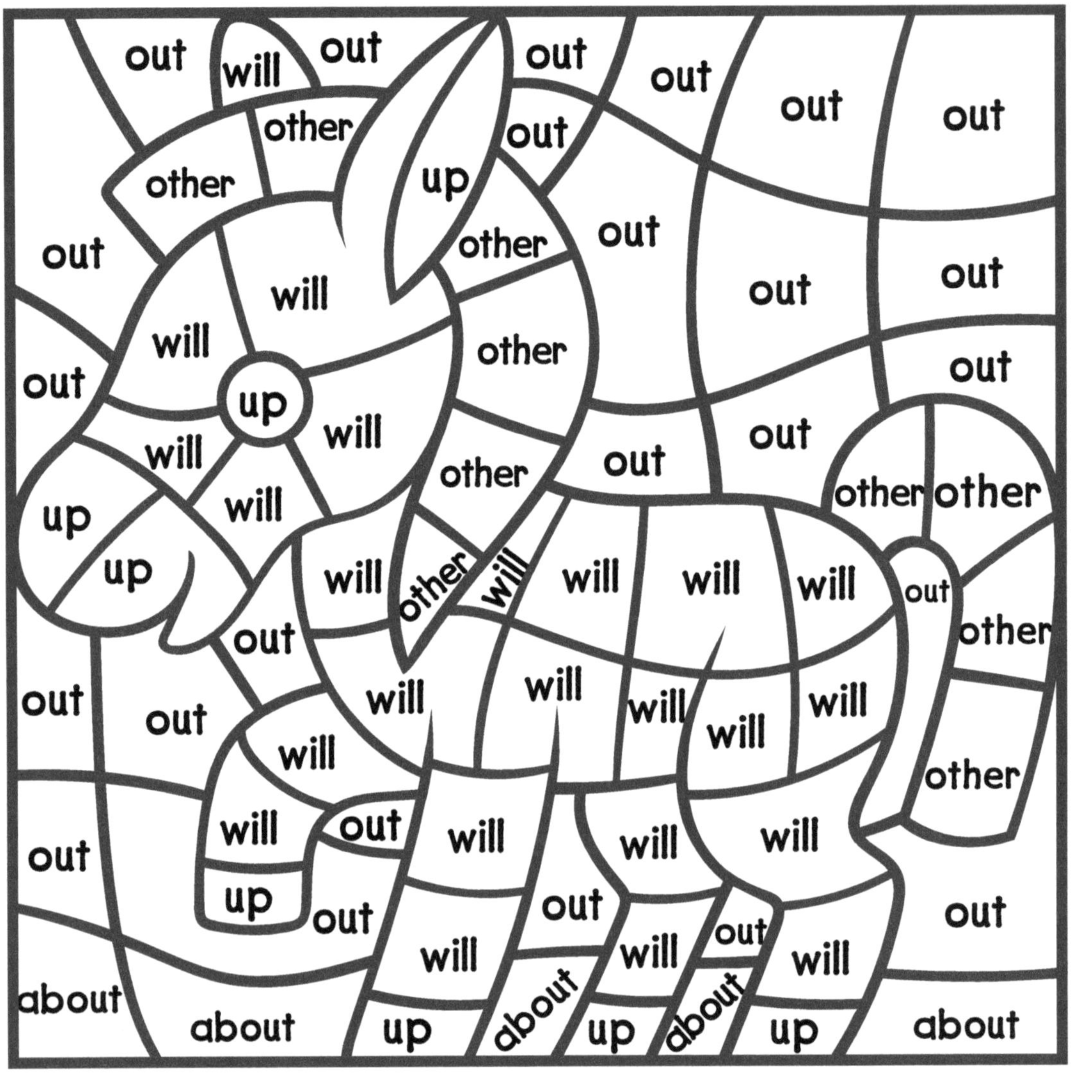

Legend

will	orange
up	black
other	brown
about	green
out	blue

2 Read the sentence. Use the legend to circle the sight words.

a) Will it rain?

b) Look up at the sky.

c) What about the other days?

d) I will look out for the rain.

e) When will the sun come out?

Sight Words: *many, then, them, these, so*

1 Read the sight words. Use the legend to colour the sight word.

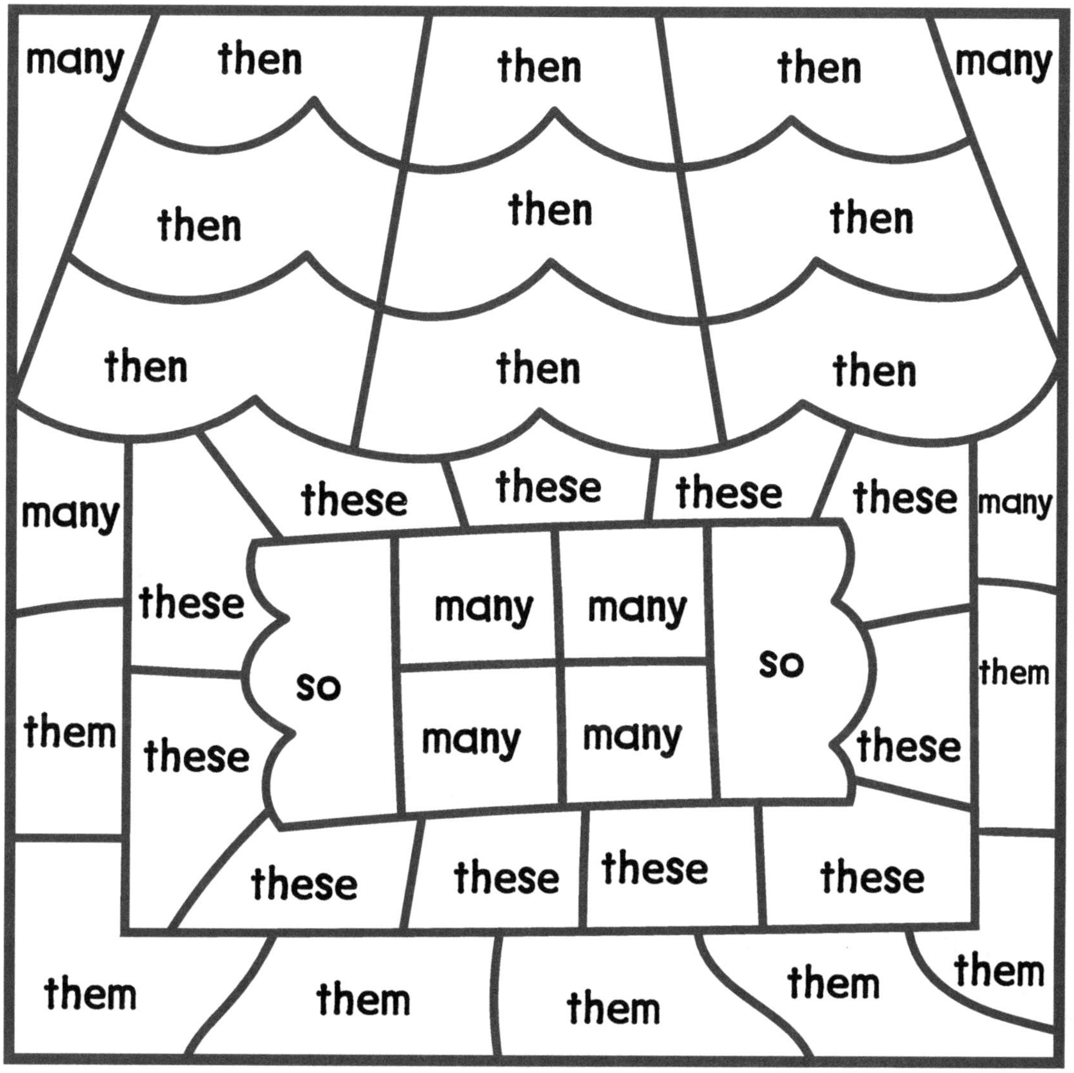

Legend

many — blue

then — red

them — green

these — orange

so — purple

2 Read the sentence. Use the legend to circle the sight words.

a) Many toys are here.

b) Then pick one.

c) I like them all!

d) These toys are so much fun!

e) So let's play with them!

Sight Words: *some, her, would, make, like*

1 Read the sight words. Use the legend to colour the sight word.

Legend

some	red
her	brown
would	green
make	blue
like	orange

2 Read the sentence. Use the legend to circle the sight words.

a) Some ducks are here.

b) Her duck is yellow.

c) Would you feed them some corn?

d) Make some ducks quack.

e) I like ducks.

Sight Words: *him, into, time, has, look*

1 Read the sight words. Use the legend to colour the sight word.

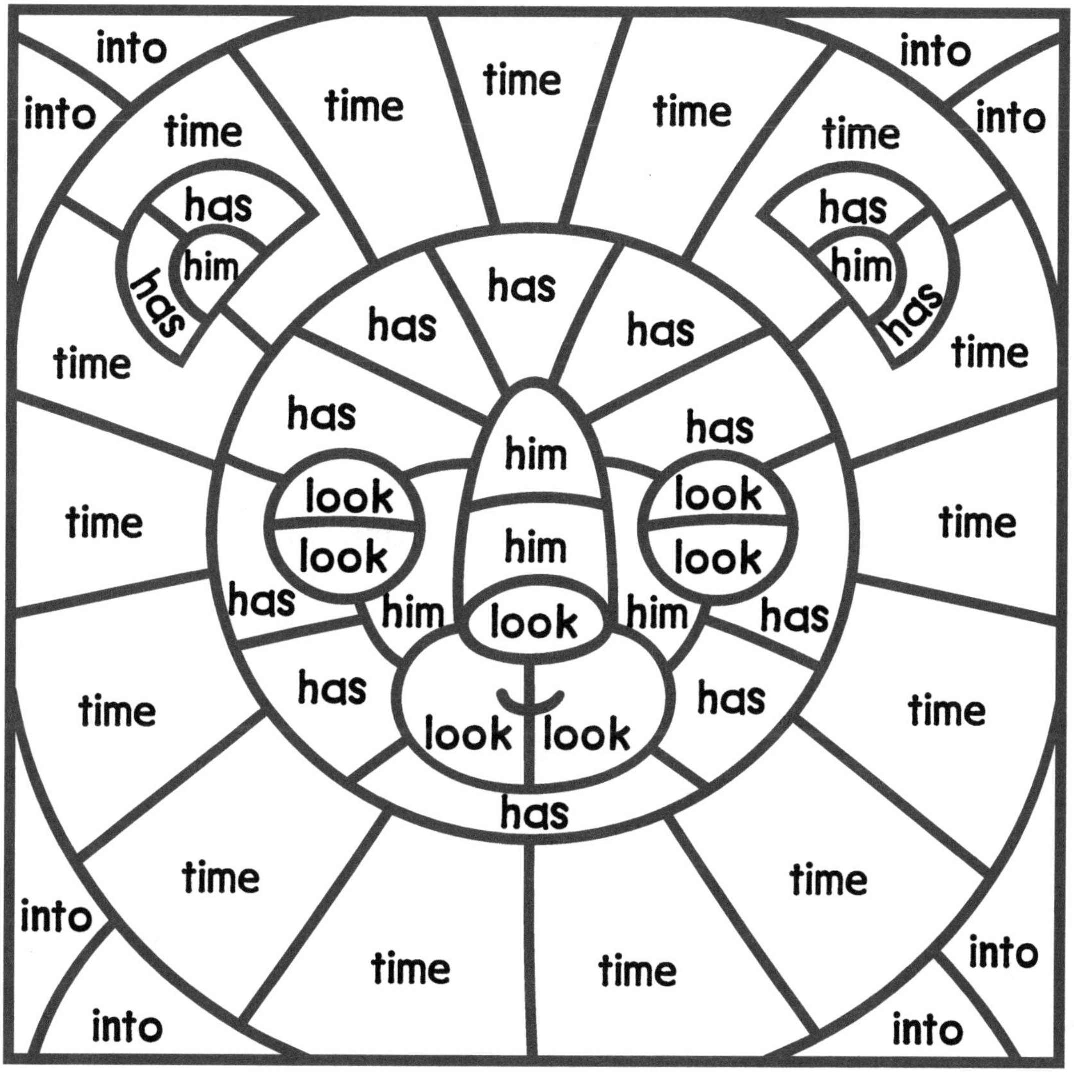

Legend

- him — brown
- into — blue
- time — orange
- has — yellow
- look — black

2 Read the sentence. Use the legend to circle the sight words.

a) What time is it?

b) Time for him to sleep.

c) He gets into the bed.

d) He has a teddy bear with him.

e) Look, he is sleeping.

Sight Words: *two, more, write, go, see*

1 Read the sight words. Use the legend to colour the sight word.

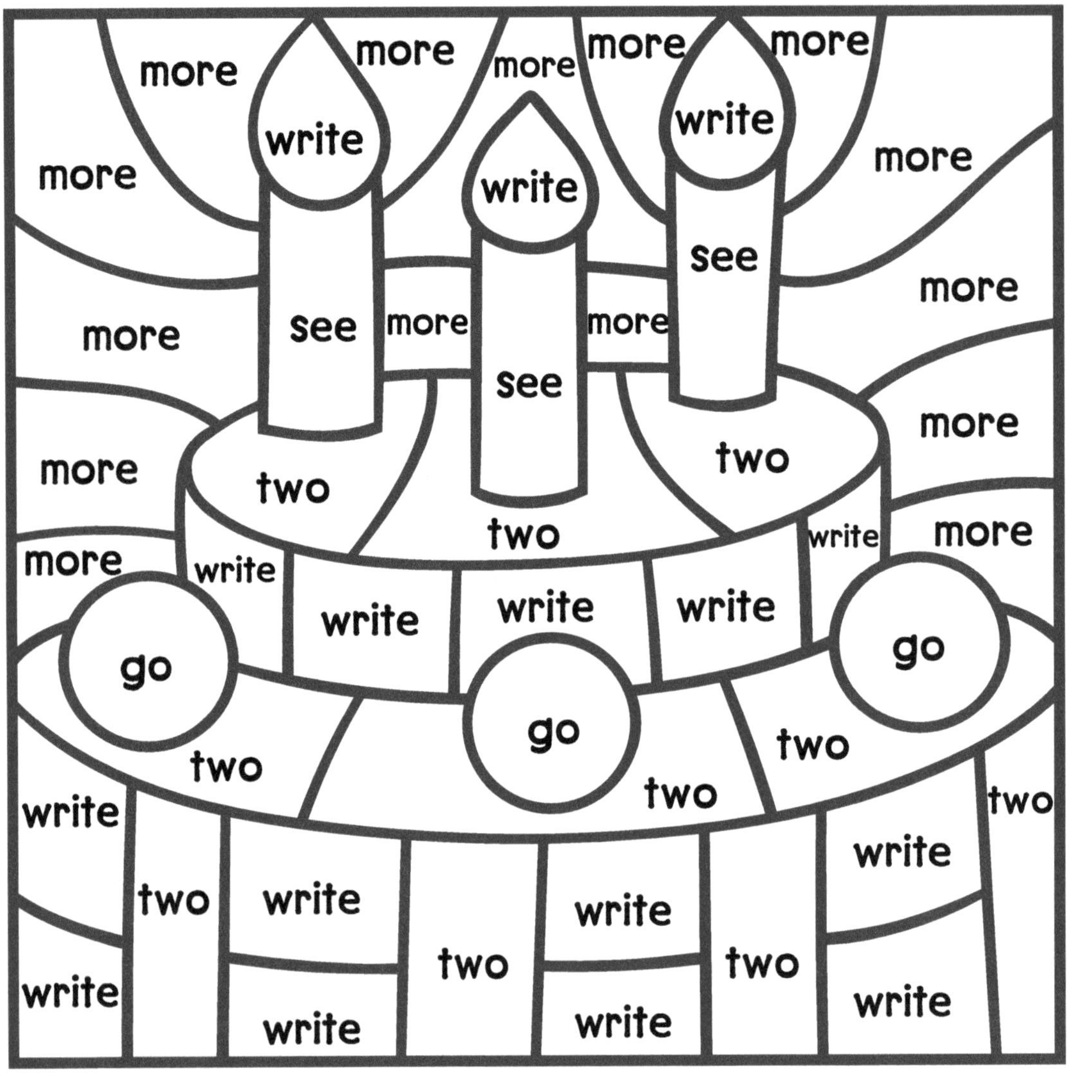

Legend

two	more	write	go	see
brown	purple	orange	red	yellow

2 Read the sentence. Use the legend to circle the sight words.

a) Time to go to school.

b) Two bags are ready.

c) Do you want more snacks?

d) Write your name on the bag.

e) Let's go see your teacher.

Sight Words: *number, no, way, could, people*

1 Read the sight words. Use the legend to colour the sight word.

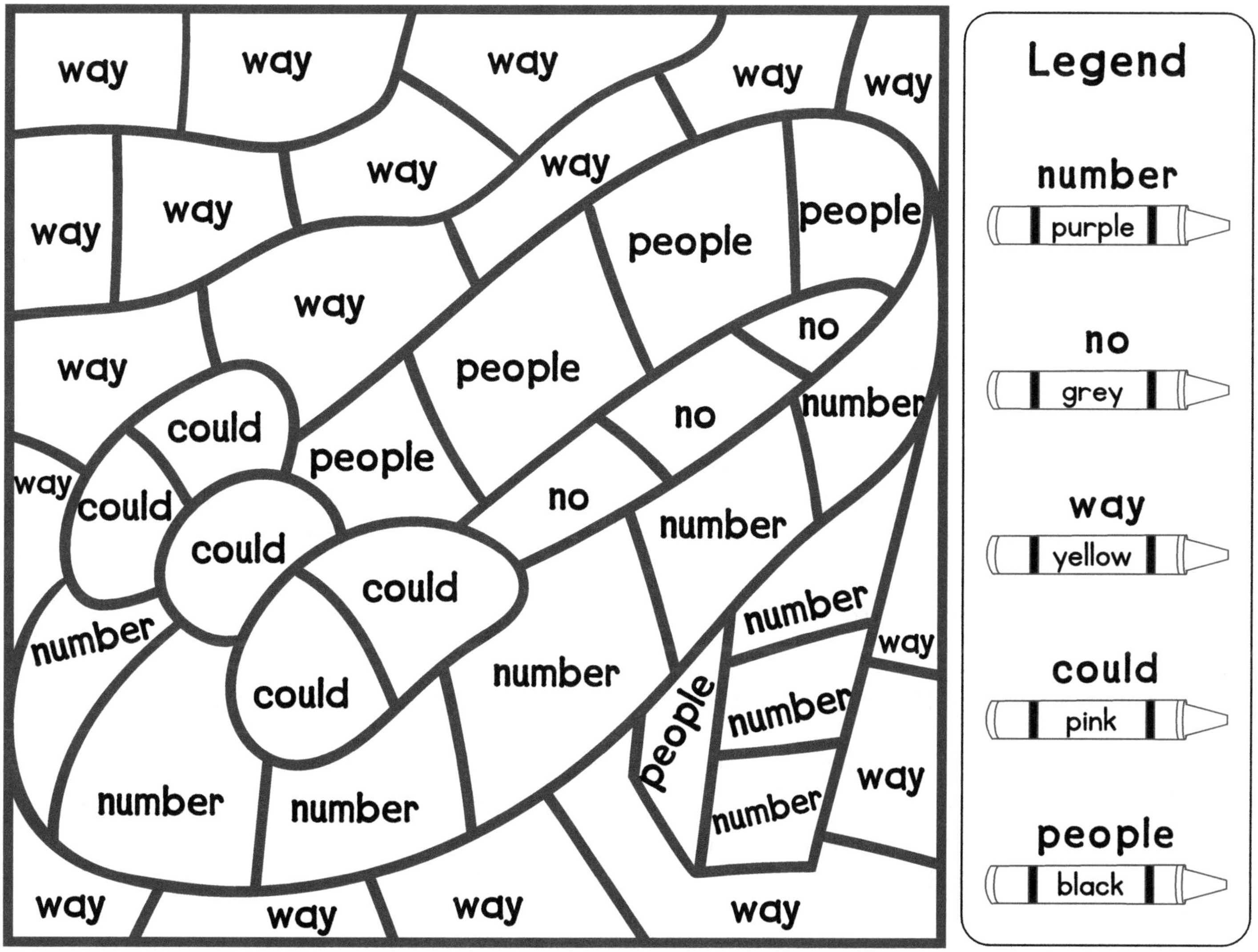

2 Read the sentence. Use the legend to circle the sight words.

a) Pick a number.

b) No way, not two!

c) Could you try again?

d) Yes, just one number!

e) People are clapping.

Spelling Word List

List 1	List 2	List 3	List 4	List 5	List 6	List 7	List 8
bag	an	at	in	box	bus	bed	fox
cab	can	bat	it	dog	cup	hen	gas
jam	fan	cat	kid	log	nut	jet	hut
map	man	hat	lip	mop	rug	leg	mug
pad	pan	mat	pig	pot	sun	net	pin
van	ran	rat	sit	rod	tub	pen	web

List 9	List 10	List 11	List 12	List 13	List 14	List 15	List 16
ape	bike	bone	bee	art	ball	hay	by
cake	dime	home	feed	bark	fall	pay	cry
face	fire	joke	he	car	mall	play	dry
game	hive	note	me	farm	tell	say	fly
gate	ice	pole	see	jar	well	stay	my
wave	tire	rose	we	star	yell	way	sky

List 17	List 18	List 19	List 20	List 21	List 22	List 23	List 24
boat	ant	dish	blow	fast	bath	book	boot
coat	hand	fish	flow	most	math	cook	food
goat	kind	she	grow	nest	that	foot	moon
load	pond	shell	low	stay	they	hook	room
road	want	ship	show	still	this	look	too
toad	went	wash	snow	stop	with	took	zoo

List 25
brown
cow
down
gown
town
wow

Try writing a funny sentence using the words from each spelling word list.

Ideas to Practice Spelling Words

Colour Code	Rainbow Words	Hidden Words
Write out your spelling words using one colour for the vowels and another colour for the consonants.	Write out your spelling words into the shape of a rainbow using the colours of the rainbow.	Draw a picture outline. Add your spelling words to the picture so they are "hiding." Colour your picture.
Cut It Out!	**Word Search**	**Rhyming Words**
Cut letters out of a magazine. Spell out your words and glue them onto a sheet of paper.	Create a word search based on your spelling words.	Write out your spelling words with a rhyming word next to each of the spelling words.
Alphabetical Order	**Spelling Word Typing**	**Magnetic Letter Words**
Print your spelling words in alphabetical order.	Type your spelling words on a computer or other device.	Use magnetic letters to make your spelling words.
Spelling Race	**Sort It Out**	**Spelling Word Fun**
How many times can you write out your spelling words in three minutes?	Sort your spelling words into categories of your choice and record them on a piece of paper.	Form your spelling words using: • modelling clay • pipe cleaners • toothpicks

Unit 1

What Is a Sentence?

A **sentence** is a group of words that tells a complete idea.

A **sentence** always begins with a **capital letter**.

✔ This is a sentence: **The dog runs fast.**

✖ This is not a sentence: **Fast dog.**

1. Circle the examples that are sentences.

a) I see a dog.

b) The apple is.

c) What is.

d) This is my sister.

2. Every sentence begins with a capital letter.
Write the sentence correctly.

my cat is cute. 

3. Write a sentence about the picture.

Exploring Kinds of Sentences

. A **telling** sentence ends with a **period**.
Examples: I have a pet. We are going to the park.

? An **asking** sentence ends with a **question mark**.
Examples: Do you have a pet? Is it a dog?

! An **exclamation** sentence shows a **strong feeling** or **excitement** and ends with an **exclamation mark**.
Examples: I love my pet! Wow! Ouch!

! . A **command** sentence tells someone to do something. It can end with a **period** or with an **exclamation mark**.
Examples: Feed your pet. Watch out!

Write the correct end mark at the end of the sentence.

1. Do you want a drink ________
2. Please sit down ________
3. Yay ________
4. When is your birthday ________
5. It is sunny outside ________

Unit 2

Making a Noun Collage

A **noun** is a word that names a person, place, or thing.

Create a noun collage.

Cut out pictures from magazine or flyers that show nouns.

Glue them into the correct category.

People
Places
Things

Am I a Person, Place, or Thing?

A **noun** is a word that names a person, place, or thing.

teacher

museum

truck

beach

books

firefighter

school

shoes

hospital

bananas

doctor

chef

cheetah

park

flower

singer

Circle the **people**. red
Circle the **places**. blue
Circle the **things**. green

Can you name more **people**.?
Can you name more **places**?
Can you name more **things**?

Proper Nouns Need a Capital Letter

Nouns that always begin with a capital letter are called **proper nouns**.

The names of **people** and **pets** begin with a capital letter.

Dr. Hill	John	Ms. Chang	Mrs. Jones
Fluffy	Sara	Mr. Smith	Benji

The names of **specific places** begin with a capital letter.

Canada	Oak Road	Adams Park
Vancouver	Ontario	Carling Arena

Days of the week and **months** begin with a capital letter.

May	Monday	Friday	March
November	Thursday	July	Saturday

Holidays and **special days** begin with a capital letter.

Canada Day	Remembrance Day	Labour Day
Halloween	Thanksgiving	Family Day

Proper Nouns Need a Capital Letter (cont.)

1 Use proper nouns to complete the sentence.

a) My friend's name is ______________________.

b) I live in ______________________.

c) The day of the week is ______________________.

2 Identify proper nouns.

Circle the **names of people** and **pets**. red

Circle **specific places**. blue

Circle **names of weekdays** or **months**. green

Circle **holidays** and **special days**. yellow

Friday	John	Ontario	Canada Day
Oak Road	Thanksgiving	November	Mr. Smith

Plural Nouns

A **plural noun** names more than one person, place, or thing.

Add **s** to most nouns to make them plural.

Example: cat ⟶ **cats**

1 Write the **plural** form of the noun by adding **s**.

a) toy ____________ b) star ____________

c) frog ____________ d) wall ____________

e) cow ____________ f) kid ____________

Some **nouns** use a new word to name **more than one**.

2 Write the correct word to name more than one.
Use the word box for help.

a) person ____________

b) tooth ____________

c) goose ____________

WORD BOX

- teeth
- geese
- people

More Plural Nouns

A **plural noun** names **more than one** person, place, or thing.

Add **es** to nouns that end with **sh**, **ch**, **x**, or **s**.

Examples: *dish* → **dishes**
watch → **watches**
mix → **mixes**
glass → **glasses**

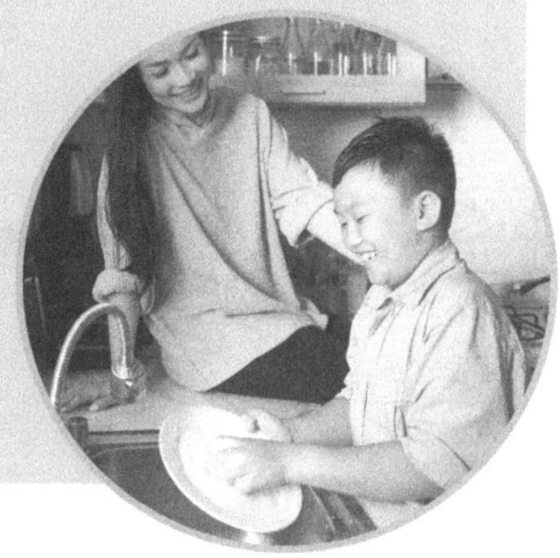

Write the **plural** form of the noun by adding **es**.

1 fox ____________

2 bush ____________

3 match ____________

4 dress ____________

5 wish ____________

6 box ____________

7 peach ____________

8 glass ____________

Compound Words

Two small words that join together to make a new word are called **compound words**.

rain

+

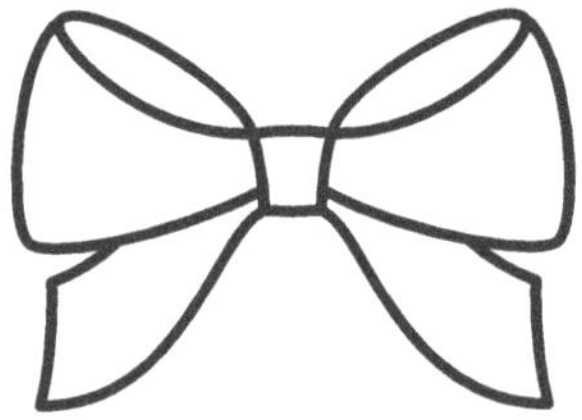

bow

=

rainbow

1 Write the **compound word**.

a)

door

+

bell

= ______________________

b)

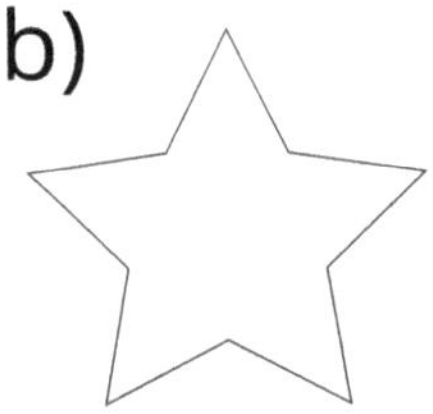

star

+

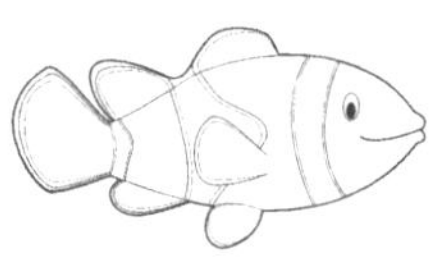

fish

= ______________________

c)

cow

+

boy

= ______________________

Compound Words (cont.)

2 Write the compound word.

a)

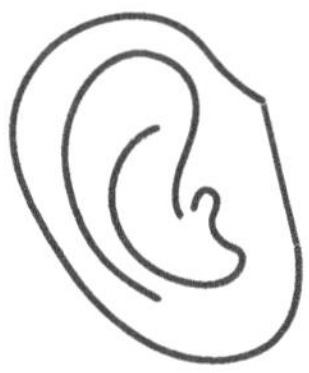 +  = ______________________

ear ring

b)

 +  = ______________________

pan cake

c)

 +  = ______________________

snow man

d)

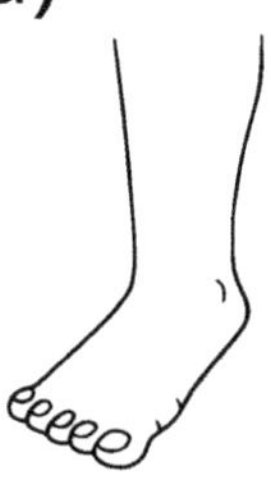 +  = ______________________

foot ball

More Compound Words

1 Draw a line from an object on the left to an object on the right to make a compound word.

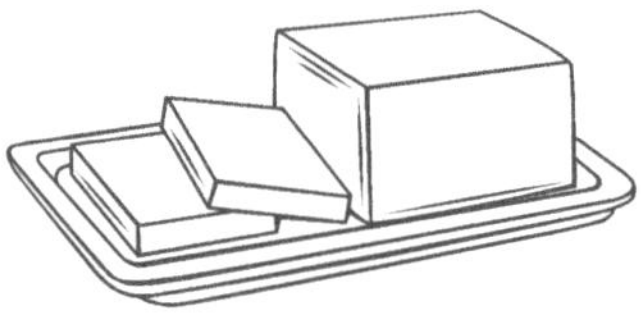

butter

cake

cup

snake

sand

fly

rattle

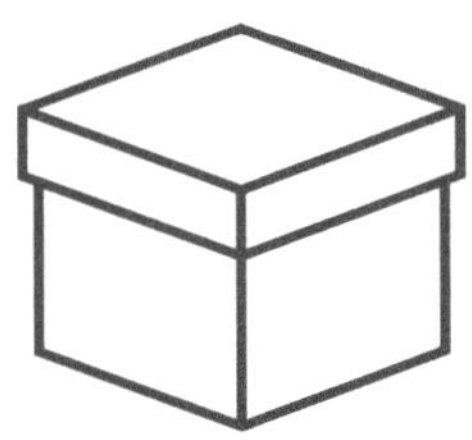

box

More Compound Words (cont.)

2 Draw a line from an object on the left to an object on the right to make a compound word.

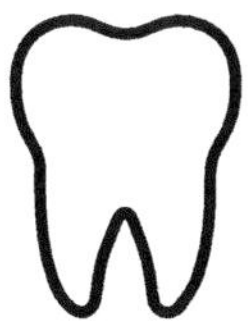

tooth

house

cat

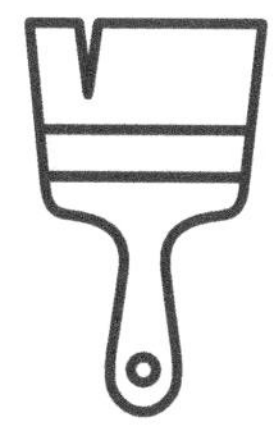

brush

doll

berry

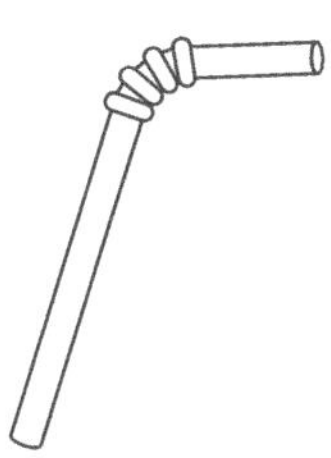

straw

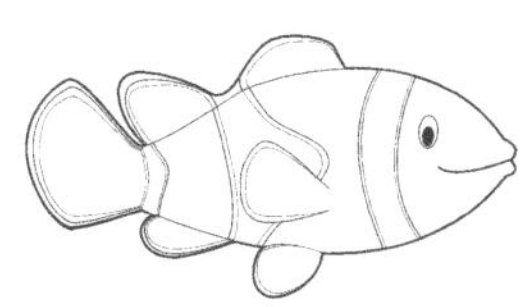

fish

Verbs Are Action Words

A **verb** is an action word that tells what happens.

Example: Tia ***jumps*** *high.* ⟶ The action word is ***jumps***.

1 Read the sentence. Print the action word.

a) The frog hops. ______________

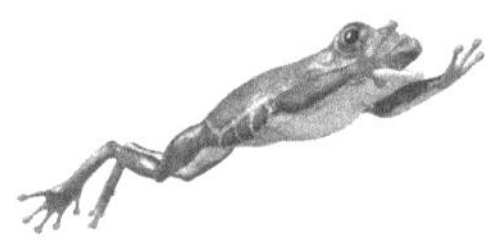

b) The baby cries. ______________

c) The dog sits. ______________

2 Draw a picture for the action sentence below.

The kids run and chase the ball.

Verb Maze

Colour the **verbs** to help the dog find the path to its house!

jumps	blue	apple	Joseph
runs	dances	book	flower
school	laughs	swims	cat
lemon	green	eats	Anna
library	mom	talks	plays

Unit 4

Adjectives

An **adjective** is a describing word.

A describing word tells a detail about a person, place, or thing.

*Examples: She has a **red** ball.* ⟶ The describing word is ***red***.

*The boy is **happy**.* ⟶ The describing word is ***happy***.

1 Read the sentence. Print the describing word.

a) The blue ball pops.

b) The soft cat purrs.

c) The food is spicy.

d) The boy is funny.

2 Write sentences using describing words.

Adjective Poem

Use **adjectives** that describe frogs to fill in the poem. Decorate your poem.

Frogs!

Frogs, frogs, frogs,

______________________ **frogs,**

______________________ **frogs,**

______________, ______________, **frogs,**

______________________ **frogs,**

I ______________________ **frogs!**

Reading Strategies

Use these helpful tips when you get stuck on a word. Colour the pictures.

Eagle Eye

Look at the picture.

What is in the picture that starts with the beginning letter sound?

Lips the Fish

Get your mouth ready!

Say the beginning letter sound right away.

Chunky Monkey

Break the word into chunks and small words you know!

B ag   Fl ag

Re-Tryin' Lion

Re-read the sentence.

Think, *"What makes sense?"*

Reading Strategies (cont.)

Use these helpful tips when you get stuck on a word. Colour the pictures.

Stretchy Snake

Slowly stretch each letter sound to read the word.

s - t - r - e - t - c - h

Skippy Squirrel

Skip the tricky words. Read to the end.

Go back and try to re-read the words.

Flippy Dolphin

Flip the vowel sounds. If the short vowel sound does not work, try the long vowel sound.

Careful Chameleon

Carefully read the whole word. Think about the word parts.

Think, *"What makes sense?"*

Reading Comprehension

Help your child develop and reinforce essential reading comprehension skills.

Before Reading - Make Predictions

- What do you think the story/text will be about? Use pictures as clues.

During Reading - Check for Understanding

Author's Purpose

- Is the author trying to persuade, inform, or entertain the reader? How do you know?

Story Structure

- Is this text fact or fiction?
- What is this reading/story/text mostly about?
- Where does the story take place?
- Who is the teller of the story? How do you know?
- Who are the characters? How are they important to the story?
- What is the problem in the story?

After Reading - Responding to the Text

- If you could give this text another title, what would be?
- Retell the story in your own words.
- What happened in the beginning/middle/end of the story?
- Who is your favourite character?
- Did you like the ending of the story? Tell why or why not.
- Which parts of the story could/could not happen in real life?

Making Connections

- How does the text they are reading remind the reader about what they already know?

Text-to-Self	Text-to-Text	Text-to-World
How does this text relate to your own life?	How is this text similar or different from something you have read before?	What does this text remind you of in the real world?

Nonfiction Text Features

Text features help the reader to understand the text better.
Here is a list of text features with a brief explanation on how they help the reader.

Feature	Explanation	Example
Table of Contents	Here the reader will find a list that provides the page numbers of the contents of the text.	Chapter 1....page 1 Chapter 2....page 5 Chapter 3....page 9
Heading	Here the reader will find a title of a section that lets the reader know what the section is about.	**Dogs** ← Dogs are a favourite pet to have.
Glossary	Here the reader will find a list of words that have definitions of what those words mean.	Dogs Cats
Diagram and Illustration	A diagram will show the reader an image that shows the parts of something. An illustration shows a drawing of an object.	
Label	A label tells the reader the title of a map, a diagram, or an illustration. Labels also draw attention to the details of a picture.	
Caption	Captions are words that are placed underneath the illustrations. Captions give the reader more information about the map, diagram, or illustration.	
Map	Maps help the reader understand where something is happening. It is a visual representation of a location.	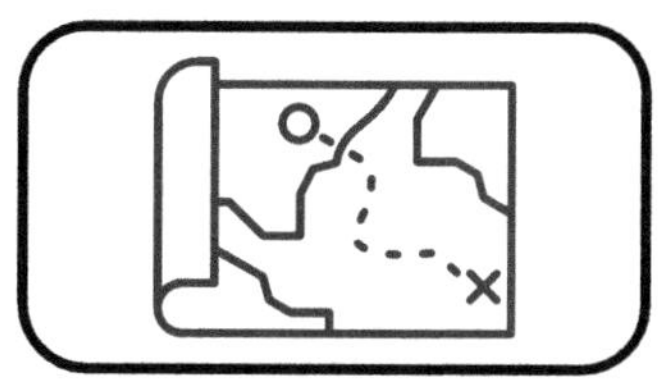
Fact Box	A fact box tells the reader extra information about the topic.	I have three dogs. Fact Box! Dogs are the most popular pet!

Text Structure

<table>
<tr><td>Cause & Effect</td><td>A cause is what makes something happen.
The effect is what happens because of the cause.

</td></tr>
<tr><td>Compare & Contrast</td><td>Compare and contrast text is a type of writing that tells how two things are alike (compare) and how they are different (contrast).
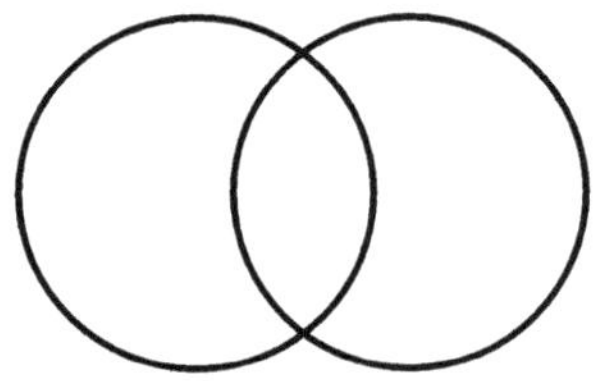</td></tr>
<tr><td>Descriptive</td><td>Descriptive writing uses words to create a picture in your mind. It helps us imagine how things look, feel, sound, and even smell!

</td></tr>
<tr><td>Procedure</td><td>A procedure text is like following a step-by-step guide.
It helps us understand the order of events and how things happen.

</td></tr>
<tr><td>Problem & Solution</td><td>This text tells about a problem that needs to be fixed.
It also shows ways to fix the problem. These are called solutions.
</td></tr>
</table>

Text Structure (cont.)

<table>
<tr><td>Informative</td><td>An informative text helps us learn about a topic by giving us facts and details.
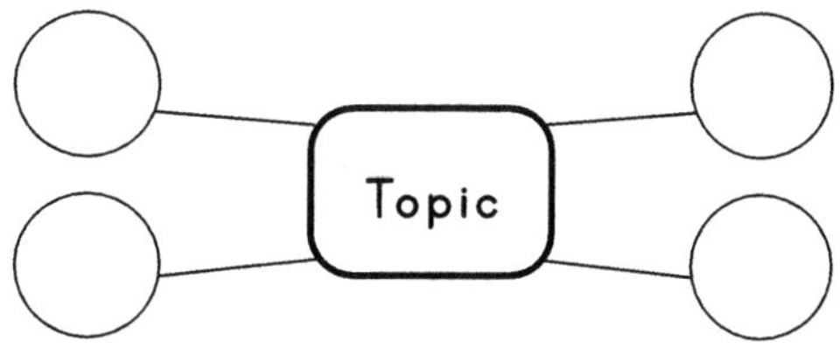
</td></tr>
<tr><td>Narrative</td><td>Narrative text is a type of writing used to tell a story. It can be a real story about something that happened or it can be a made up story!
</td></tr>
<tr><td>Persuasive</td><td>Persuasive writing tries to convince someone to agree with an idea or to do something. The writer does this by giving good reasons and examples in their writing.
</td></tr>
<tr><td>Biography</td><td>A biography is a text that tells true and interesting facts about a person's life.
</td></tr>
<tr><td>Recount</td><td>A recount text pattern is a type of writing that tells about something that happened, often in the order it happened, with details and sometimes personal thoughts or feelings.
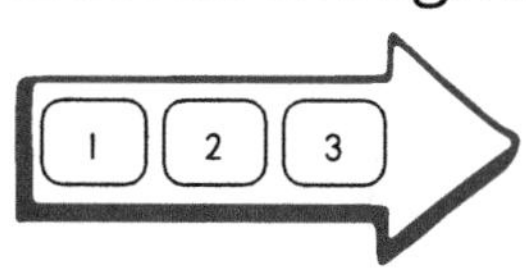
</td></tr>
</table>

Cats and Dogs

Cats and dogs are pets, but they are different.

Cats are small and do things alone.

Dogs are many sizes and love to be with people.

Cats purr. Dogs wag their tails.

Cats use a litter box. Dogs go outside.

Cats clean themselves. Dogs need baths.

Both are good friends to us, but have special things about them.

A cat washing its paw

A dog having a bath

Colour the **title**. yellow Colour the **caption**. orange

Cats and Dogs – Think About It!

1. Which sentence best describes the main idea of the text?

   a) Cats are better than dogs.
   b) Dogs are better than cats.
   c) Cats and dogs are different but both make good pets.

2. What do you think dogs do when they are happy?

   a) purr   b) wag their tails   c) clap

3. What does the picture of the cat in the text help you understand?

   a) cats clean themselves   b) cats purr

4. Have you ever noticed these differences between cats and dogs in real life? Share with a friend.

   YES   NO

5. How do cats and dogs show they are happy?

● purr

● wag their tails

Cats and Dogs – Think About It! (cont.)

6 Use the Venn Diagram to show how cats and dogs are the same and different.

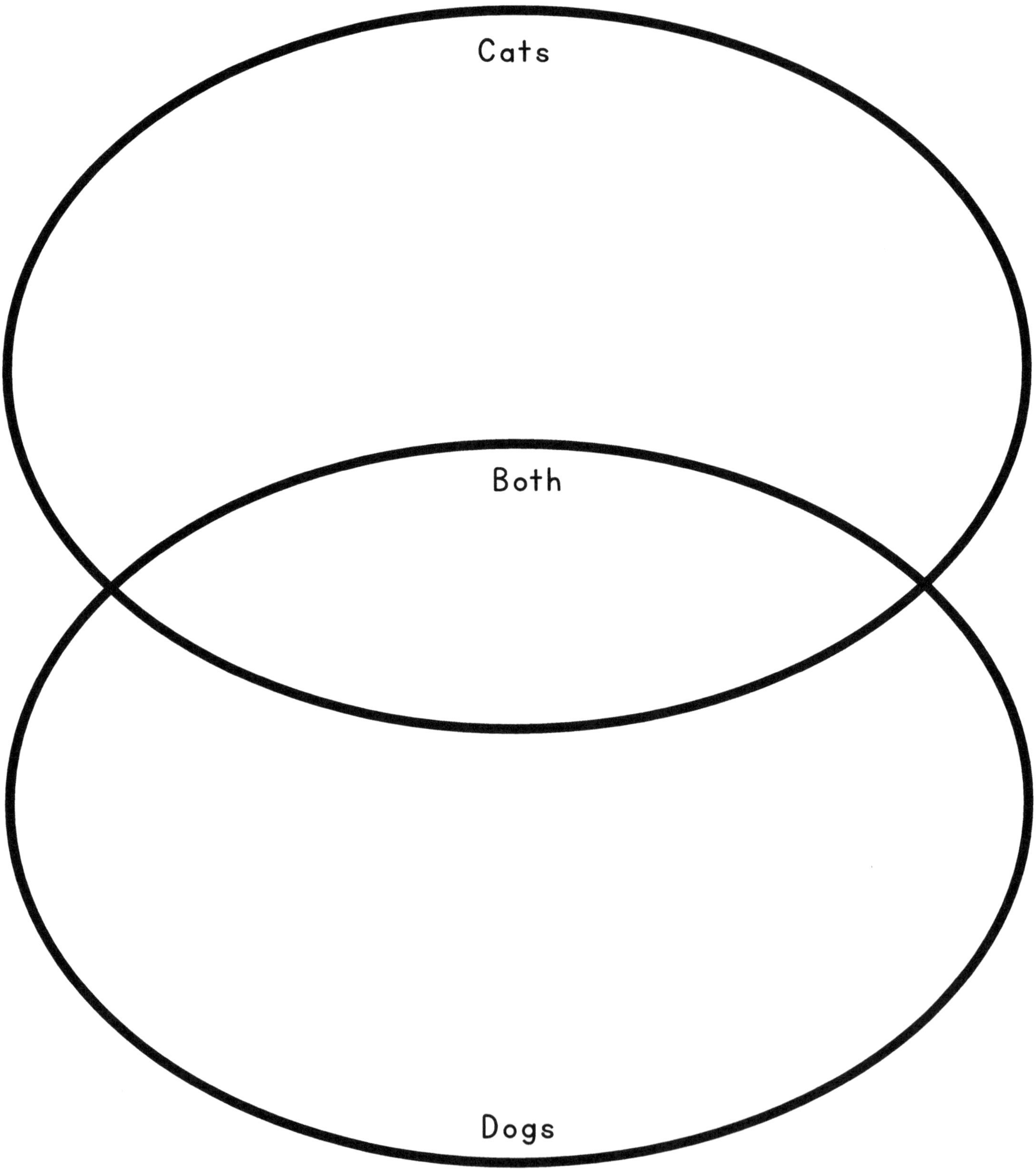

Cats and Dogs – Think About It! (cont.)

7. Draw a picture of a cat doing things alone and a dog loving to be with people. Write one sentence for each to explain what they are doing in the picture.

Draw a picture.

☐ I used capitals and end marks. ☐ My printing is neat. ☐ My writing makes sense.

Narrative

Cleaning Your Room

Mom said, “Let’s clean your room!”

So we picked up toys and put them in bins.

Then, we put books on the shelf.

Mom dusted the furniture, and I swept the floor.

Now, our room looks tidy.

Mom was happy, and we felt proud.

Cleaning our room made us feel good inside.

Mom and child clean the room

Colour the **title**. blue Colour the **caption**. yellow

Cleaning Your Room – Think About It!

1. Who is telling the story?

   a) Mom b) Child

2. Who said, "Let's clean your room!"

   a) Mom b) Child

3. Fill in the blank using words from the story.

clean	dusted	picked	put	swept

a) Mom said, "Let's ______________ your room!"

b) So, we ______________ up toys.

c) Then, we ______________ books on the shelf.

d) Mom ______________ the furniture.

e) I ______________ the floor.

Cleaning Your Room – Think About It! (cont.)

4 Why was it important to put the toys in bins?

a) to sell them later
b) to make the room look neat
c) to take them to school

5 How did Mom and the child feel after cleaning the room?

a) sad and disappointed  b) happy and proud 

6 Why do you think Mom and the child felt good inside after cleaning?

a) because they found lost toys
b) because the room looked tidy
c) because they didn't have to clean anymore

7 What does this story remind you of? Share your thinking.

Cleaning Your Room – Think About It! (cont.)

8. What might the child and Mom do next after cleaning the room?

Draw a picture.

☐ I used capitals and end marks. ☐ My printing is neat. ☐ My writing makes sense.

Our Day

First, we went to the park to play.

Then, we flew our kites in the open sky.

Next, we played tag.

After that, we ate ice cream to cool off.

Finally, we went home, happy and tired.

Kids flying a kite

Colour the **words in the story that let us know the order of things that happened.** yellow

Our Day – Think About It!

1. What is the main idea of the story?

    a) eating ice cream
    b) having a fun day at the park
    c) flying kites

2. Which word in the story shows a type of feeling?

    a) sky b) ice cream c) happy d) tag

3. Why do you think the children were able to fly their kites in the open sky?

    a) because it was raining
    b) because it was windy
    c) because it was snowing

4. Number these activities in the order they happened in the story.

    ________ We ate ice cream to cool off.

    ________ We played tag.

    ________ We flew our kites in the open sky.

Our Day – Think About It! (cont.)

5 Circle **True** or **False**.

a) They went to the park to swim. True False

b) They felt tired at the end of the day. True False

c) They ate ice cream to cool off. True False

d) The first thing they did was fly kites. True False

6 Draw a picture of what you like to do at the park.

Write a sentence about your drawing.

Our Day – Think About It! (cont.)

7. Complete the five senses poem about the park. Decorate your poem.

AT THE PARK

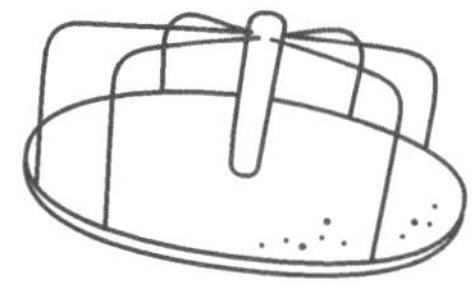

I see... ______________________________

I hear... ______________________________

I smell... ______________________________

I feel... ______________________________

I taste... ______________________________

Informative

Who Provides My Food?

Farmers grow food.

They sow seeds and care for plants.

Farmer with vegetables

They pick fruits and vegetables.

Farmers take care of animals.

Chickens give eggs and meat.

Cows give milk and meat.

Truck drivers take the food to stores.

Store clerks sell the food.

Colour the **title**. blue Colour the **caption**. pink

Who Provides My Food? – Think About It!

1 What kind of text is this?

a) fiction b) nonfiction

2 What is the main idea of the text?

a) How farmers take care of animals.
b) What truck drivers do.
c) How people work together to grow and sell food.

3 What does the word “sow” mean in the text?

a) to plant seeds
b) to pick fruits and vegetables
c) to sell food

4 Why do you think farmers care for plants?

a) to make the plants happy
b) to help the plants grow big and strong
c) to play with the plants
d) to give them water

Who Provides My Food? – Think About It! (cont.)

5. Why is it important for store clerks to sell the food?

   a) so they can eat it
   b) so they can become farmers
   c) so the food doesn't go bad

6. Which animals mentioned provide both eggs and meat?

   a) chickens   b) cows   c) pigs   d) sheep

7. Draw lines to connect each job to its correct description.

Job	Description
 Farmer	This person sells the food.
 Truck Driver	This person transports food to stores.
 Store Clerk	This person sows seeds, grows food, and cares for plants.

Who Provides My Food? – Think About It! (cont.)

Cut and paste a picture of fruits and vegetables to sell.
Complete this advertisement to convince people to buy them.

FRUIT AND VEGETABLE STAND

Contact me at:

Selling price:

Let me tell you why!

☐ I used capitals and end marks. ☐ My printing is neat. ☐ My writing makes sense.

A Hole in My Sock

This morning I saw a tiny hole in my sock.

My socks have the letter “L” on the sides.

“L” stands for Lucy and that is my name.

At school, the hole got big.

I put some tape over it.

At lunch time, the tape came off.

When I walked home, my big toe was showing.

Oh no! The hole is too big to fix now.

Goodbye sock!

Lucy looks at her sock

Colour the **title**. red Colour the **caption**. orange

A Hole in My Sock – Think About It!

1. What does the letter "L" stand for on the girl's sock?

2. What problem does Lucy have in the story?

   a) She can't find their other sock.
   b) She is hungry.
   c) There's a hole in her sock.

3. What does Lucy use to try to fix the hole in her sock?

   a) glue   b) tape   c) paint

4. Why did Lucy put tape on the hole in her sock?

   a) to make it look pretty
   b) to keep her foot warm
   c) to fix the hole for a little while

5. What is the lesson from the story "A Hole in My Sock"?

   a) Take good care of your things and try to fix them.
   b) Throw away your old socks.
   c) Never wear socks with holes.

A Hole in My Sock – Think About It! (cont.)

6 Find and circle the words in the word search puzzle.

FIX	HOLE	HOME	LUCY
LUNCH	SOCK	TAPE	TOE

H	O	M	E	V	T
O	L	Z	P	R	A
L	U	C	Y	J	P
E	N	X	T	O	E
G	C	S	O	C	K
V	H	Y	F	I	X

A Hole in My Sock – Think About It! (cont.)

7 Colour and decorate the sock. Describe your sock.

My sock is...

☐ I used capitals and end marks. ☐ My printing is neat. ☐ My writing makes sense.

Can We Get a Dog?

Dear Mom and Dad,

Can we get a dog?

Every dog needs a good home.

We can get one at the shelter.

I promise to take care of it.

I will feed it.

I will walk it.

I will play with it.

I will pick up after it.

A dog is a good pet for us to love.

Your son,
Andrew

Can We Get a Dog? – Think About It!

1. What is Andrew trying to get his parents to do?

2. What did Andrew write to his parents?

   a) a poster b) a letter c) a story

3. Where can Andrew's family get a dog?

   a) at the store b) at the park c) at the shelter

4. What are three good reasons that Andrew uses?

5. Do you think Andrew got a dog? Tell why.

Can We Get a Dog? – Think About It! (cont.)

6 Draw lines from the actions Andrew promises to the correct descriptions.

Feed it ●	● Be a friend and have fun
Walk it ●	● Clean up its mess
Play with it ●	● Give it food
Pick up after it ●	● Take it outside for exercise

7 Write about the picture of Andrew taking care of his pet.

8 How do you think Andrew would feel the moment his parents agree to get a dog?

a) sad

b) angry

c) excited

d) bored

Can We Get a Dog? – Think About It! (cont.)

9 Create a post of Andrew and his new dog.

☐ I used capitals and end marks. ☐ My printing is neat. ☐ My writing makes sense.

The Day My Cat Spoke

One morning, my cat Abby climbed up on my bed and said, “Get up, Ben.”

“Did you just tell me to get up, Abby?” I asked.

“Yes. If you do not hurry, you will be late for school,” said Abby.

I jumped out of bed. “Thanks, Abby.”

“Meow,” said Abby. “See you later.”

My cat talked! It was wonderful!

Abby and Ben

Colour the **title**. green Colour the **caption**. red

The Day My Cat Spoke – Think About It!

1. Is the story about Ben and his cat Abby fiction or nonfiction?

   a) fiction (made-up stories)
   b) nonfiction (real stories)

2. What is the cat's name in the text?

   ____

3. How do you think the boy felt when he heard his cat talk?

   a) surprised    b) upset    c) bored 

4. What did the cat tell Ben to do?

   ____

5. What does the word "wonderful" mean in the sentence, "My cat talked! It was wonderful!"?

   a) terrible   b) boring   c) amazing

The Day My Cat Spoke – Think About It! (cont.)

6 What does the word “jumped” mean in the sentence, “I jumped out of bed”?

a) stayed in bed

b) got out of bed quickly

c) slept for a long time

7 Draw lines to match the person to what they said in the story.

Ben

Abby

“Get up, Ben.”

“Did you just tell me to get up, Abby?”

8 Do you think this story can happen in real life? Explain.

The Day My Cat Spoke – Think About It! (cont.)

9. Imagine a cat just spoke to you and your friend. Write what everyone said.

Ice Cream Fun

Do you like ice cream?

Make an ice cream sundae.

Here is what you do:

- First, put some ice cream into a bowl.

- Then, pour some syrup on it.

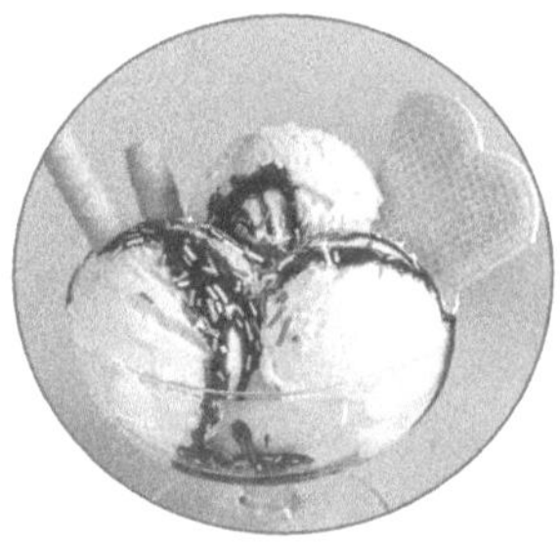

- Next, add some toppings.

- Finally, eat the ice cream!

Colour the **question** in the text. red
Colour the **title**. orange

Ice Cream Fun – Think About It!

1 Draw lines from the order to the steps to make a sundae.

First, ●	●	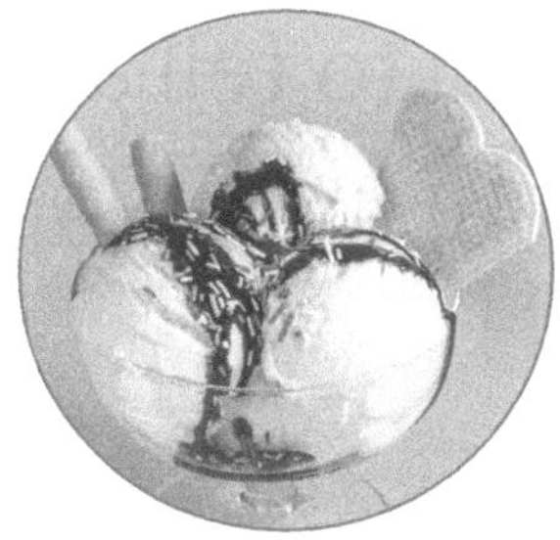 add some toppings.
Then, ●	●	 eat the ice cream!
Next, ●	●	 pour some syrup on it.
Finally, ●	●	 put some ice cream in a bowl.

Ice Cream Fun – Think About It! (cont.)

2 What is the purpose of this text?

a) to tell a story about a day at the park

b) to explain how to make an ice cream sundae

3 Sort the words into the chart.

add	bowl	eat
ice cream	pour	syrup

Nouns	Action Words

Ice Cream Fun – Think About It! (cont.)

4. Create your own sundae. Draw a picture and describe your sundae.

Pretend you are eating your sundae.

How does it look?

How does it smell?

How does it taste?

Other details:

☐ I used capitals and end marks. ☐ My printing is neat. ☐ My writing makes sense.

My Pet Fish

I have two pet fish.

Every day, I give them food.

The fish need food to stay alive.

My fish swim up and eat the tiny flakes.

I make sure I feed my fish.

Feeding them is fun.

I like to watch my pet fish.

A girl with her fish

Colour the **title**. orange Colour the **caption**. yellow

My Pet Fish – Think About It!

1. What kind of pets does the author have at home?

   a) cats b) dogs c) fish d) birds

2. How do the fish eat their food?

   a) they use a fork
   b) they swim up and eat tiny flakes
   c) they ask the author to feed them

3. How often does the author give food to their fish?

   a) every day b) once a week

A **cause** is why something happens.
An **effect** is what happens because of the cause.

4. Match the **Cause** to its **Effect**.

Cause	Effect
The fish need food to stay alive.	I make sure I feed my fish.
	The fish stay healthy.

Hamsters and Rabbits

Many children have a hamster or a rabbit for a pet.

They are both small animals. They are also very different.

Hamsters

hamster

Hamsters eat meat and vegetables. They are active at night. They like to be alone. Sometimes they bite so you have to be careful if you have them for a pet.

Rabbits

rabbit

Rabbits only eat vegetables. They like people. They don't usually bite. They usually live longer than hamsters.

Colour the **headings**. blue Colour the **captions**. yellow

Hamsters and Rabbits – Think About It!

1. **True** or **False**? Hamsters and rabbits are big animals.

   a) True   b) False

2. Which pet can sometimes bite?

   a) hamsters   b) rabbits

3. Which pet likes people more?

   a) rabbits   b) hamsters

4. Which word in the text tells us that hamsters can be awake and do things when it is dark?

   a) night   b) alone   c) active

5. Are hamsters most active in the daytime or at night?

   a) daytime    b) night 

6. If you have vegetables at home, which pet can you feed them to?

   a) hamster   b) rabbit   c) both

Hamsters and Rabbits – Think About It! (cont.)

7. Use the Venn Diagram to show how hamsters and rabbits are the same and different.

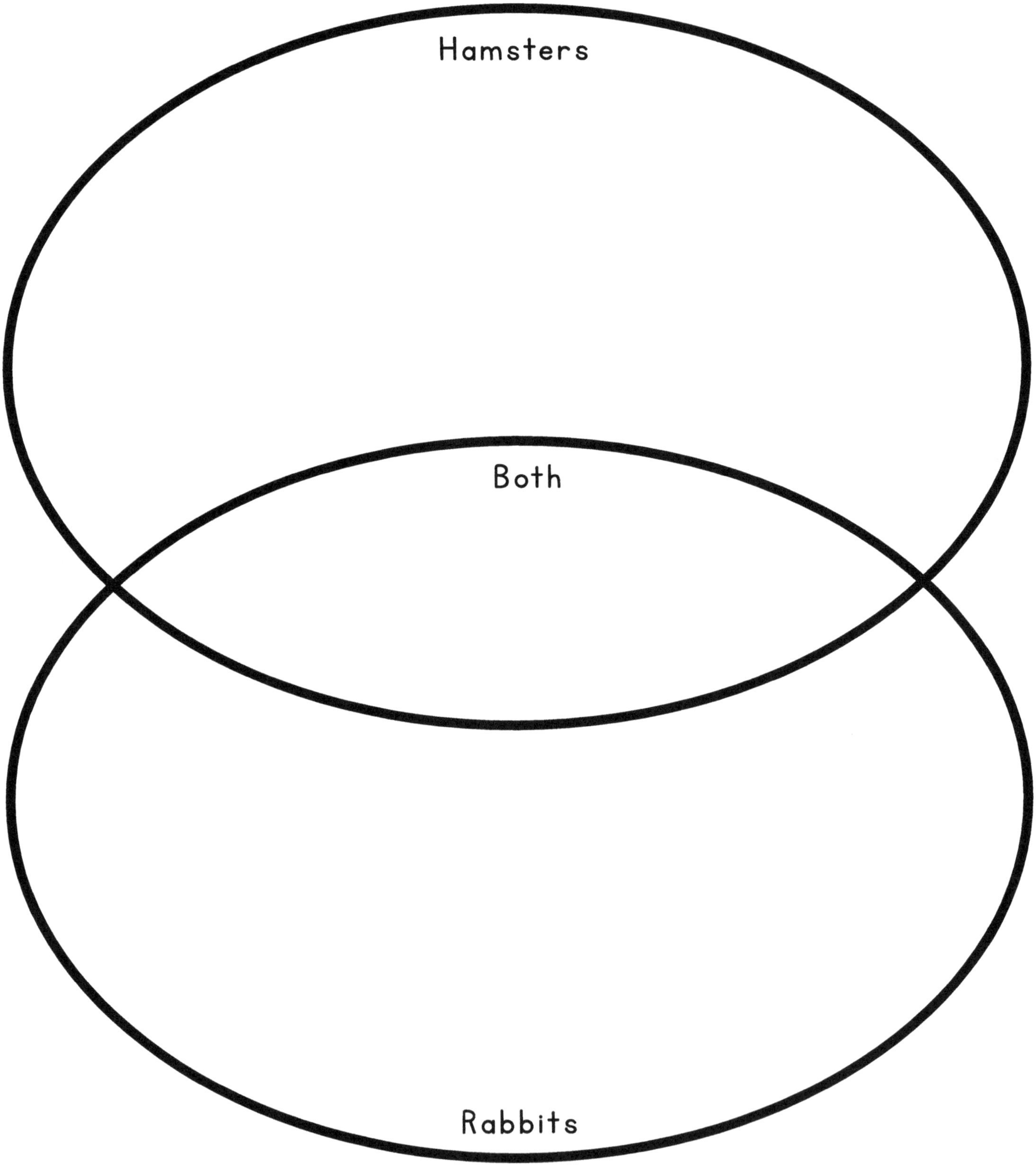

Hamsters and Rabbits – Think About It! (cont.)

8 Would you rather have a hamster or a rabbit?

I would rather have a ______________________

Let me tell you why.

☐ I used capitals and end marks. ☐ My printing is neat. ☐ My writing makes sense.

My Pet Bird

I have a pet bird.

It is the size of my hand.

It lives in a cage. The cage has a branch.

The bird sings a lot, like a happy song.

It eats seeds.

My bird has bright, shiny feathers.

Some are green, and some are blue.

What's a good name for my pet bird?

Bird in its cage

Colour the **title**. orange Colour the **caption**. blue

My Pet Bird – Think About It!

1 What is the purpose of this text?

a) to tell a story about a bird's adventure
b) to describe the author's pet bird

2 Fill in the blank using words from the story.

bird	cage	feathers	hand	seeds

a) I have a pet ______________________ .

b) It is the size of my ______________________ .

c) It lives in a ______________________ .

d) It eats ______________________ .

e) My bird has bright, shiny ______________________ .

My Pet Bird – Think About It! (cont.)

3 What is a good name for the pet bird?

4 Look at the picture. How does the girl feel?

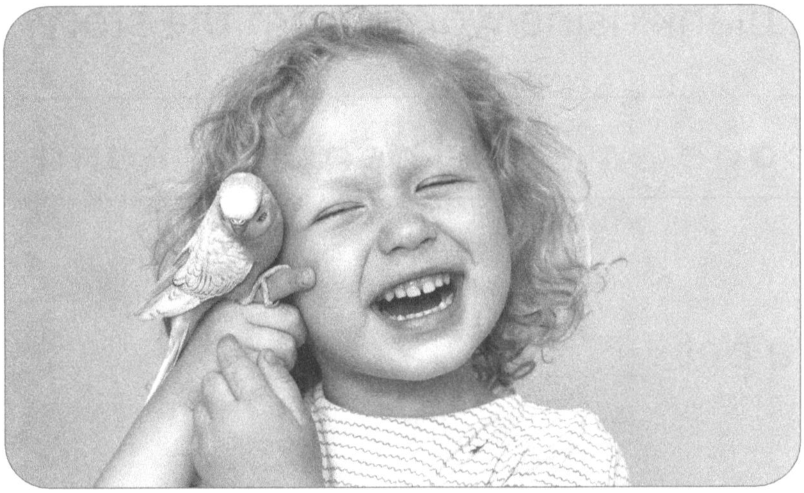

a) happy

b) sad

c) angry

5 What does this text remind you of?

My Pet Bird – Think About It! (cont.)

An **acrostic poem** is a poem in which the first letters of each line spell out a word or message.

B

I

R

D

☐ I used capitals and end marks. ☐ My printing is neat. ☐ My writing makes sense.

Sidney Crosby

Sidney Crosby is a hockey player.

He is one of Canada's best.

Sidney was born in 1987.

Two years later, he began playing hockey.

When Sidney was just 18, he joined the National Hockey League.

He soon became captain of his team.

"Sid the Kid" works hard.

He is a good skater.

He has a great shot.

Colour two facts. red Colour the title. yellow

Sidney Crosby – Think About It!

1 Who is Sidney Crosby?

a) a writer
b) a hockey player
c) a painter

2 Fill in the blank using words from the box.

best	hard	hockey	shot	skater

a) Sidney Crosby is a ________________ player.

b) He is one of Canada's ________________ .

c) "Sid the Kid" works ________________ .

d) He is a good ________________ .

e) He has a great ________________ .

Sidney Crosby – Think About It! (cont.)

3. Who is telling us about Sidney Crosby?

   a) Sidney Crosby b) someone else

4. What year was Sidney Crosby born?

   a) 1987 b) 1997 c) 2007

5. Can you remember a time when you tried very hard to do something, like Sidney Crosby does in hockey? Explain.

6. What is Sidney Crosby's nickname?

7. Do you have a nickname?

Sidney Crosby – Think About It! (cont.)

8 Pretend you are going to meet Sidney Crosby. What question will you ask him?

☐ I used capitals and end marks. ☐ My printing is neat. ☐ My writing makes sense.

Reading Log – Books I Have Read

Book Title	Purpose of the Text	Rate This Book
	☐ to inform ☐ to entertain ☐ to persuade	☆ ☆ ☆ ☆
	☐ to inform ☐ to entertain ☐ to persuade	☆ ☆ ☆ ☆
	☐ to inform ☐ to entertain ☐ to persuade	☆ ☆ ☆ ☆
	☐ to inform ☐ to entertain ☐ to persuade	☆ ☆ ☆ ☆
	☐ to inform ☐ to entertain ☐ to persuade	☆ ☆ ☆ ☆
	☐ to inform ☐ to entertain ☐ to persuade	☆ ☆ ☆ ☆

Making Connections After Reading

Book Title: ______________________________

After reading...	It reminds me of...	This helps me make a connection to...
	something else I have read something about me the world around me	
	something else I have read something about me the world around me	

My Connection After Reading

Book Title: ___

This book reminds me of: something else I have read | something about me | the world around me

Let me tell you why.

☐ I used capitals and end marks. ☐ My printing is neat. ☐ My writing makes sense.

Nonfiction Report

Topic: ______________________________

Draw and label a picture about your topic.

Here are some facts I learned:

☐ I used capitals and end marks. ☐ My printing is neat. ☐ My writing makes sense.

Story Report

Title: ______________________________

Author: ______________________________

Illustrator: ______________________________

Who is the **main character** in the story? This is who the story is mostly about.

____

Draw the **main character** from the story.

Is this your favourite character?

☐ yes

☐ no

List three words to **describe** the **main character**.

____

Story Report

Where does the story take place? This is called the **setting** of the story.

Draw a picture of the **setting**.

What is the **problem** in the story?

How does the story end? How is the **problem solved**?

Story Map

Title: ____

Characters

Setting

Beginning

Middle

End

Reading Response

Title: ____

This book is: ☐ Fiction ☐ Non-Fiction

Draw a picture of your favourite part of the book.

Rate this book!
☆ ☆ ☆ ☆

This is my favourite part of the book. Let me tell you why.

☐ I used capitals and end marks. ☐ My printing is neat. ☐ My writing makes sense.

Fact and Opinion

I read about this topic: ____________________________________

✓ **Fact** A statement that can be proven to be true.
Opinion A feeling or belief about something.

☐ I used capitals and end marks. ☐ My printing is neat. ☐ My writing makes sense.

Missing!

Contact me at:

Reward

Who or what:

When last seen:

Where last seen:

Description:

☐ I used capitals and end marks. ☐ My printing is neat. ☐ My writing makes sense.

How to Take Care of a Pet!

Draw a picture of your pet.

This is how to take care of a pet:

1.

2.

3.

My pet is special because...

☐ I used capitals and end marks. ☐ My printing is neat. ☐ My writing makes sense.

My Journal About...

☐ I used capitals and end marks. ☐ My printing is neat. ☐ My writing makes sense.

Recount Writing Planner

Who?

What?

When?

Where?

Why?

My Recount About the Best Day Ever!

The best day ever was when...

First,

Then,

Last,

This day made me feel...

☐ I used capitals and end marks. ☐ My printing is neat. ☐ My writing makes sense.

All About My Visit to ____________________

When did you go? Who did you go with? What was it like?

☐ I used capitals and end marks. ☐ My printing is neat. ☐ My writing makes sense.

All About ______________________________

What did you do? Who did you do it with? What was it like?

☐ I used capitals and end marks. ☐ My printing is neat. ☐ My writing makes sense.

I Should Stay Up Late!

Convince your babysitter to let you stay up late.

I should have a later bedtime. Let me tell you why.

First of all,

Another reason is,

Finally,

This is why I should have a later bedtime!

☐ I used capitals and end marks. ☐ My printing is neat. ☐ My writing makes sense.

Congratulations!

Great Work!

Answers

Beginning Letter Sounds pp. 4–7

1. a) dog, duck b) jellyfish, jar c) question, quilt d) map, mouse e) piano, panda

2. a) f b) y c) v d) b e) w

3. a) a b) t c) i d) h e) s f) x g) u h) g i) z

4. a) c b) s c) k d) r e) b f) n g) l h) e i) o

Beginning Letter Sounds: Rhyming pp. 8–9

1. a) hat b) pen c) sit d) bug e) dog

2. a) bed b) car c) pig d) pot e) sun

Ending Letter Sounds pp. 10–11

1. a) m b) g c) t d) x e) n f) l g) k h) f i) r

2. a) k b) l c) d d) w e) b

Beginning and Ending Letter Sounds p. 12

1. hat **2.** corn **3.** lion **4.** net **5.** leaf **6.** pool

Consonant Blends with *s* pp. 14–17

1. a) sc b) sn c) sp d) st e) sl f) sk g) sn h) st i) sk

2. a) sw b) sl c) sn d) st e) sk f) sw g) sk h) sm i) st

3. a) st b) sl c) sp d) sm e) sc f) sn

4. a) sp b) sw c) sc d) sk e) sm f) sl

Consonant Blends with *r* pp. 18–21

1. a) br b) tr c) cr d) pr e) gr f) tr g) cr h) fr i) br

2. a) dr b) cr c) br d) tr e) fr f) pr g) cr h) dr i) tr

3. a) pr b) fr c) br d) dr e) cr f) gr

4. a) fr b) br c) cr d) tr e) gr f) pr

Consonant Blends with *l* pp. 22–25

1. a) fl b) gl c) pl d) cl e) bl f) cl g) pl h) gl i) bl

2. a) bl b) cl c) gl d) fl e) pl f) bl g) pl h) gl i) cl

3. a) fl b) bl c) pl d) gl e) cl f) fl

4. a) cl b) fl c) gl d) pl e) fl f) bl

More Consonant Blends pp. 26–27

1. a) cr b) sn c) pl d) sp e) fr f) gl

2. a) tr b) sl c) dr d) sk e) pl f) st

Words with *sh* pp. 28–29

1. a) sheep b) ship c) brush d) fish e) shell

2. shark, shovel, shoe **3.** a) shell b) shop

Words with *th* pp. 30–31

1. a) thread b) path c) think d) bath e) thumb

2. tooth, three, sloth

3. a) with b) they

Short and Long Vowels pp. 32–33

1. well, leaf **2.** jam, tape **3.** pie, fish **4.** tub, cube **5.** coat, dog **6.** fan, cave **7.** net, tree **8.** dice, milk **9.** phone, lock

Short Vowel Practice: *a* pp. 34–35

1. a) map b) van c) bat d) cap e) jam f) fan

2. a) plant b) rabbit c) calf

3. a) camel b) mask

Short Vowel Practice: *e* pp. 36–37

1. a) bell b) net c) web d) tent e) jet f) well

2. a) hen b) fence c) belt

3. a) steps b) nest

Short Vowel Practice: *i* pp. 38–39

1. a) milk b) pillow c) six d) fish e) igloo f) pig

2. a) ribbon b) dinner c) kid

3. a) dig b) bin

Short Vowel Practice: *o* pp. 40–41

1. a) fox b) doll c) moth d) pot e) lock f) rod

2. a) log b) top c) frog

3. a) otter b) box

Short Vowel Practice: *u* pp. 42–43

1. a) tub b) drum c) nut d) truck e) lunch f) mug

2. a) sucker b) button c) bug

3. a) bus b) jug

Long Vowel Practice: *a* pp. 44–45

1. a) gate b) tape c) cave d) plane e) game f) mane

2. a) grapes b) cage c) snake d) rake e) ape

Long Vowel Practice: *e* pp. 46–47

1. a) feet b) meal c) bee d) seal e) deer f) steam

2. a) jeans b) leaf c) cheese d) key e) tree

Long Vowel Practice: *i* pp. 48–49

1. a) bike b) hive c) dime d) kite e) nine f) dice

2. a) lion b) fire c) pie d) slide e) tire

Long Vowel Practice: *o* pp. 50–51

1. a) bowl b) stove c) rose d) note e) cone f) goat

2. a) snow b) phone c) home d) boat e) rope

Long Vowel Practice: *u* pp. 52–53

1. a) cube b) music c) menu d) June e) mule f) human

2. a) tissue b) fuel c) statue d) music e) cute

***Y* as Long Vowel Sounds p. 55**

1. a) Long *e* b) Long *i* c) Long *i* d) Long *e* e) Long *i* f) Long *e* g) Long *e* h) Long *e* i) Long *i*

Answers

Words with *ai* and *ay* pp. 56–57

1. *ai* words: drain, main *ay* words: say, today

2. a) pail b) train c) spray

3. a) hay b) nail c) May d) paint e) pay

Words with *ee* and *ea* pp. 58–59

1. *ee* words: beef, peel *ea* words: beak, cream

2. a) sheep b) beach c) leaf

3. a) seeds b) feet c) seal d) tea e) cheese

Words with *ie* and *igh* pp. 60–61

1. *ie* words: cried, dried, lie *igh* words: high, might, night

2. a) light b) pie

3. a) tie b) knight c) die d) bright e) pie

Words with *oa* and *ow* pp. 62–63

1. *oa* words: goal, loaf *ow* words: grow, slow

2. a) boat b) snow c) crow

3. a) coat b) toad c) bowl d) soap e) bow

Words with *oo* and u p. 64

1. a) suit b) glue c) pool

2. a) moon b) flute c) tooth

Words with *ew, ue,* and *ui* p. 65

1. *ew* words: flew, stew *ue* words: blue, clue
ui words: fruit, suit

2. a) fruit b) jewel c) glue

Words with *oi* and *oy* pp. 66–67

1. *oi* words: join, point *oy* words: annoy, enjoy

2. a) soil b) toilet c) cowboy

3. a) boy b) toy c) coin d) boil e) noise

Words with *ow* and *ou* pp. 68–69

1. *ow* words: howl, town *ou* words: count, hour

2. a) mouse b) crown c) house

3. a) flower b) cow c) cloud d) clown e) flour

Words with *-le* p. 70

1. a) turtle b) apple c) candle d) noodle e) table
f) puddle

2. a) ble b) fle c) zle d) tle

Words with Silent Letters p. 71

1. a) k b) w c) b

2. a) comb b) write c) knife

***R*-Controlled Vowels pp. 72–75**

1. a) ar b) or c) er d) ir e) ur f) ar

2 a) or b) ir c) er d) ar e) ur f) or

3. a) er b) ar c) ur d) ir e) ur f) or

4. a) er b) ir c) or d) ar e) ur f) er

Word Families: *all* and *ell* p. 76–77

1. all words: call, fall, hall ell words: cell, fell, spell

2. a) red: ball blue: tell b) red: mall blue: yell

3. a) ball b) well c) bell

4. a) smell b) small

Word Families: *at* and *an* pp. 78–79

1. *at* words: bat, mat, pat *an* words: can, man, ran

2. a) green: cat orange: ran b) green: sat orange: man

3. a) hat b) pan c) rat

4. a) fan b) fat

Word Families: *op* and *ap* pp. 80–81

1. *op* words: drop, hop, pop *ap* words: lap, nap, zap

2. a) yellow: top blue: sap b) yellow: cop blue: nap

3. a) top b) shop c) clap

4. a) mop b) map

Word Families: *ut* and *ug* pp. 82–83

1. *ut* words: cut, gut, rut *ug* words: bug, hug, jug

2. a) orange: but purple: bug b) orange: cut purple: dug

3. a) nut b) rug c) mug

4. a) hug b) hut

Word Families: *en* and *in* pp. 84–85

1. *en* words: den, men, ten *in* words: spin, tin, win

2. a) blue: ten green: win b) blue: men green: tin

3. a) hen b) fin c) bin

4. a) pin b) pen

Word Families Review pp. 86–87

1. a) hat b) bell c) pin d) shop e) mug

2. a) ten b) jug c) tap d) pan e) wall

Words with *nd* and *nt* pp. 88–89

1. *nd* words: land, mend, send *et* words: bent, pant, want

2. a) green: kind red: went b) green: band red: sent

3. Check that the words are printed correctly.

Words with *ow* pp. 90–91

1. a) snow b) tow c) bow d) rainbow e) crow

2. flower, crown, cow

3. a) grow b) down

Words with a Short *oo* Sound pp. 92–93

1. a) foot b) cook c) wood d) book e) hook

2. a) look b) wool c) good d) woof

Answers

3.

Y	S	Z	B	P
X	T	O	O	K
F	O	O	T	V
H	O	O	D	Z
T	D	W	M	Q

Words with a Long *oo* Sound pp. 94–95

1. a) pool b) zoo c) moon d) boot e) food

2. a) room b) tool c) soon d) spoon

3.

S	C	O	O	P
P	O	V	W	X
R	O	O	F	Y
Z	L	Q	N	R
X	B	O	O	M

Prefixes p. 96

1. un **2.** dis **3.** un **4.** dis

Suffixes p. 97

1. less **2.** ful **3.** ful **4.** less

Sight Words: *the, of, and, a, to* p. 100

2. a) The b) of c) and, to d) a e) to

Sight Words: *in, is, you, that, it* p. 101

2. a) it, is, in b) You, it c) That, is d) you e) is, in, that

Sight Words: *he, was, for, on, are* p. 102

2. a) he b) was c) for d) on e) are

Sight Words: *as, with, his, they, I* p. 103

2. a) as, as b) with c) his d) they e) I

Sight Words: *at, be, this, have, from* p. 104

2. a) at b) be, at c) This d) have e) from

Sight Words: *or, one, had, by, words* p. 105

2. a) one b) or c) had d) by e) words

Sight Words: *but, not, what, all, were* p. 106

2. a) all b) all c) but, not d) what, were e) were, all

Sight Words: *we, when, your, can, said* p. 107

2. a) we b) when, can, we c) can, your d) Your e) said

Sight Words: *there, use, an, each, which* p. 108

2. a) There b) Use c) Each d) An, there e) Which

Sight Words: *she, do, how, their, if* p. 109

2. a) She b) How, she c) Their d) Do, how e) if

Sight Words: *will, up, other, about, out* p. 110

2. a) Will b) up c) about, other d) will, out e) will, out

Sight Words: *many, then, them, these, so* p. 111

2. a) Many b) Then c) them d) These, so e) So, them

Sight Words: *some, her, would, make, like* p. 112

2. a) Some b) her c) would, some d) Make, some e) like

Sight Words: *him, into, time, has, look* p. 113

2. a) time b) him c) into d) has e) look

Sight Words: *two, more, write, go, see* p. 114

2. a) go b) two c) more d) Write e) go, see

Sight Words: *number, no, way, could, people* p. 115

2. a) number b) No, way c) Could d) number e) People

What Is a Sentence? p. 118

1. a) ✓ b) × c) × d) ✓

2. My cat is cute. **3.** Answers will vary.

Exploring Kinds of Sentences p. 119

1. ? **2.** . **3.** ! **4.** ? **5.** .

Am I a Person, Place, or Thing? p. 121

Red: teacher, firefighter, doctor, chef, singer

Blue: museum, beach, school. hospital, park

Green: truck, books, shoes, bananas, cheetah, flower

Proper Nouns Need a Capital Letter pp. 122–123

1. Answers will vary.

2. Red: John, Mr. Smith Blue: Ontario, Oak Road
Green: Friday, November
Yellow: Canada Day, Thanksgiving

Plural Nouns p. 124

1. a) toys b) stars c) frogs d) walls e) cows f) kids

2. a) people b) teeth c) geese

More Plural Nouns p. 125

1. foxes **2.** bushes **3.** matches **4.** dresses **5.** wishes
6. boxes **7.** peaches **8.** glasses

Compound Words pp. 126–127

1. a) doorbell b) starfish c) cowboy

2. a) earring b) pancake c) snowman d) football

Answers

More Compound Words pp. 128–129

1.

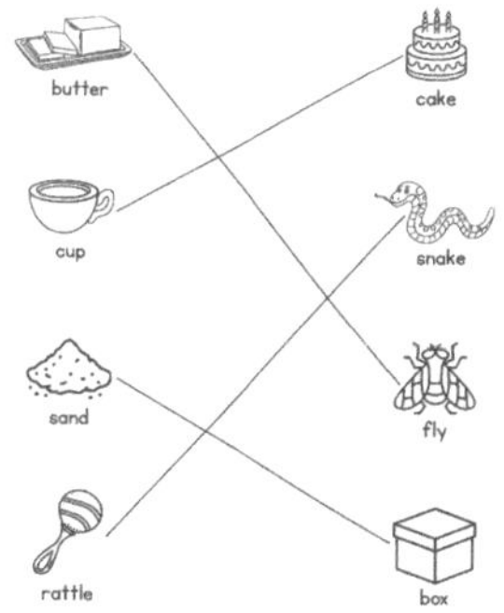

2.

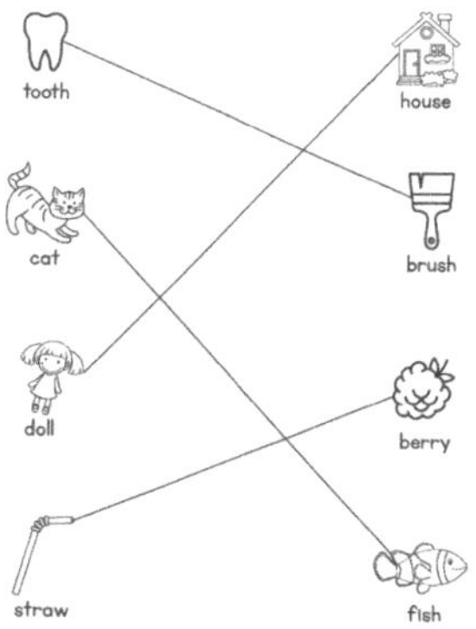

Verbs Are Action Words p. 130

1. a) hops b) cries c) sits **2.** Drawings will vary.

Verb Maze p. 131

Coloured verbs: jumps, runs, dances, laughs, swims, eats, talks, plays

Adjectives p. 132

1. a) blue b) soft c) spicy d) funny **2.** Answers will vary.

Adjective Poem p. 133

1. Answers will vary.

Cats and Dogs pp. 140–143

1. c **2.** a **3.** a **4.** Answers will vary.

5. Dogs wag tails, Cats purr

6. and 7. Answers will vary.

Cleaning Your Room pp. 144–147

1. b **2.** a

3. a) clean b) picked c) put d) dusted e) swept

4. b **5.** b **6.** b

7. and 8. Answers will vary.

Our Day pp. 148–151

1. b **2.** c **3.** b

4. 3, 2, 1

5. a) false b) true c) true d) true

6. and 7. Answers will vary.

Who Provides My Food? pp. 152–155

1. b **2.** c **3.** a **4.** b **5.** c **6.** a

7.

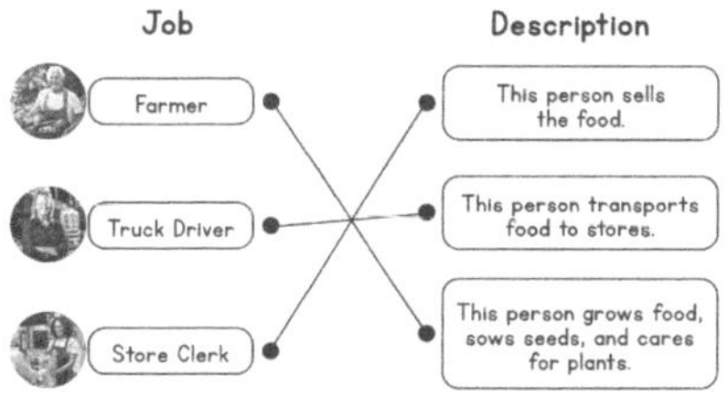

A Hole in My Sock pp. 156–159

1. Lucy

2. c **3.** b **4.** c **5.** a

6.

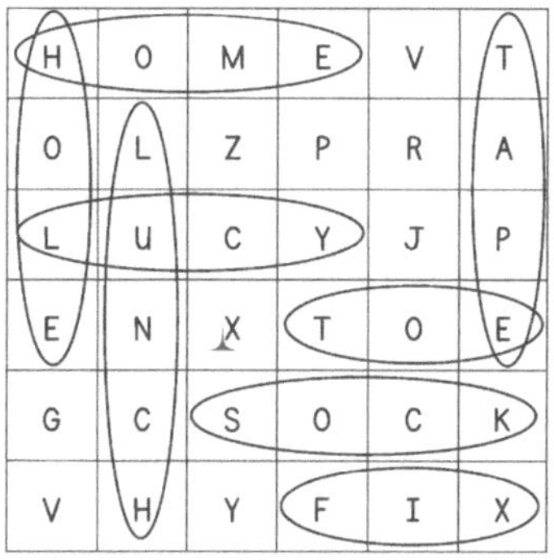

7. Answers will vary.

Can We Get a Dog? pp. 160–163

1. Get him a dog.

2. b **3.** c

4. Answers will vary. Examples: Every dog needs a good home. We can get one at the shelter. I promise to take care of it.

5. Answers will vary.

6.

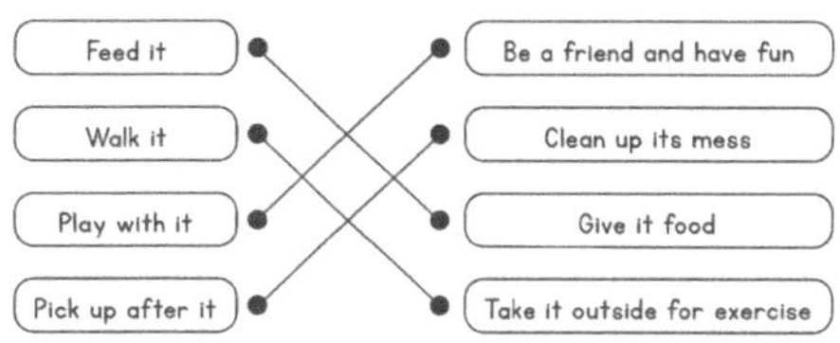

7. Answers will vary. **8.** c **9.** Answers will vary.

The Day My Cat Spoke pp. 164–167

1. a **2.** Abby **3.** a **4.** Get up.

5. c **6.** b

7. Ben - “Did you just tell me to get up, Abby?”
Abby - “Get up, Ben”

8. and 9. Answers will vary.

Answers

Ice Cream Fun pp. 168–171

1.

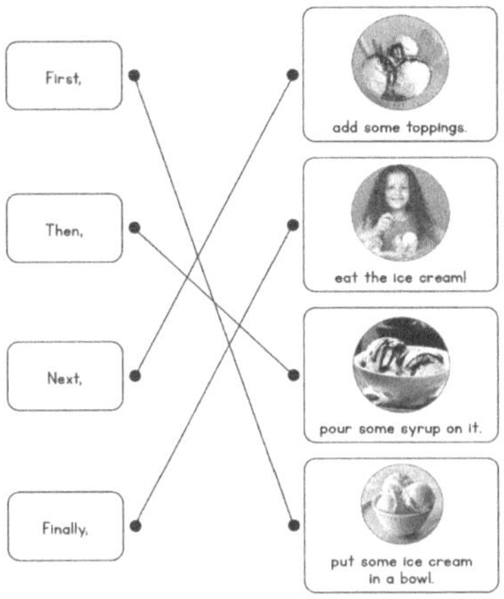

2. b

3. Nouns: bowl, ice cream, syrup
Action Words: add, eat, pour

4. Answers will vary.

My Pet Fish pp. 172–173

1. c **2.** b **3.** b

4. I make sure I feed my fish

Hamsters and Rabbits pp. 174–177

1. b **2.** a **3.** a **4.** c **5.** b **6.** c

7. and 8. Answers will vary.

My Pet Bird pp. 178–181

1. b

2. a) bird b) hand c) cage d) seeds e) feathers

3. Answers will vary.

4. a

5. Answers will vary.

Sidney Crosby pp. 182–185

1. b

2. a) hockey b) best c) hard d) skater e) shot

3. b **4.** a

5. Answers will vary.

6. "Sid the Kid"

7. and 8. Answers will vary.